My Journey Beyond Beyond

An autobiographical record
of deep calling to deep
in pursuit of intimacy with God

Mike Parsons

First published in the United Kingdom in 2018 by
The Choir Press
in conjunction with
Freedom Apostolic Ministries Ltd.

ISBN 978-1-78963-008-4 Paperback

ISBN 978-1-78963-009-1 eBook

Dedication

This book is dedicated to all those who have walked with me on this amazing journey. My mum who has faithfully prayed for me my whole life that I would serve God's purposes. My wife and family who were often sacrificed on the altar of "church" and have had to put up with a singlemindedness and dedication to not always the right causes. My fellow travellers who have walked with me along the way. The Joshua Generation who have bravely come out of the wilderness and crossed over beyond the veil into the unknown. The *Engaging God* family who have been willing to step out in pursuit of their destinies in God. Those courageous forerunners and explorers who have paved the way for others including myself to follow. Finally but not least my heavenly Father who formed me out of the desire of His heart and called me to be His son.

Acknowledgements

I wish to express my gratitude to those who have helped in the birthing of this book. The Freedom Church family who have supported me by being willing to explore this journey together despite most times not knowing where we have been going. Those who have encouraged me to write, some who prophesied, some who listened. Laure Fabre for her passion, encouragement and willingness to blog my teachings to the francophone world and proof read this book. Jeremy Westcott for carrying my heart, faithfully blogging hundreds of hours of teaching, tirelessly correcting my spelling and grammar, making sense of my ramblings and editing this book.

Contents

Introduction: The Journey Begins

As I ponder where my journey began, I remember as a child dreaming of adventures, quests and exploits of derring-do, and being drawn to films and TV programmes like Robinson Crusoe, Thunderbirds, Stingray, Lawrence of Arabia, Forbidden Planet and Lost in Space. My first book was H.G. Wells' The Time Machine, which resonated with the destiny God had agreed with my spirit in the before. That destiny was buried deep within my soul, hidden, but creating that splinter within my mind which sought to break free of the limitations of my mundane existence. I longed to go beyond the small Cornish town that framed my life but films and dreams were my only avenue.

God had wired me to be inquisitive, always curious about how things were made and how they worked. I often took things apart and, to my mother's dismay, was unable to reassemble them. I loved to try to fix things that were broken, using my inbuilt ingenuity to solve problems with whatever was at my disposal.

I often went on adventures, sometimes with my friends but mostly on my own, and would come back with some treasure - usually a creature that I had captured to be added to my personal zoo.

Throughout my life, I have resonated with the mind-expanding possibilities of science fiction, Star Wars, Star Trek, the Marvel superhero universe comics and, more recently, films. I was stirred by the adventures of Bilbo Baggins in The Hobbit as it was read to us in junior school and later as I explored the world of Middle-earth in the Lord of the Rings trilogy.

God had placed within my soul the desire for adventure that longed to be outworked but only began to find expression when I discovered that I was included in God's cosmic plan for the restoration of all things.

That deep-seated inspirational drive was at the heart of my quest for knowledge and a reality that always seemed just beyond my grasp. There was always something at the core of my being that knew there had to be more than this. "I still haven't found what I'm looking for" are the lyrics of a U2 song that I resonated with for most of my life. When I first saw the movie The Matrix I discovered that the false and fabricated reality of religion had been pulled over my eyes. I was inspired to find the truth that had been obscured by the religious veil and willing to pay whatever the cost to discover what I had always known but had never been able to see. Thus began the quest for true reality, to discover what my destiny had always been looking for.

If I were God (fortunately I am not), the religious backwater of a small town in the far southwest of the United Kingdom would not have been my choice of place to begin the journey. My destiny and calling were to be a forerunner, therefore hindrances and obstacles often characterised the path I was destined to follow. All this was of God's design, in order hopefully to inspire others that nothing is impossible with a God who often chooses the foolish things of this world.

So my journey was framed by being born and brought up in at least a semi-religious environment. My father was the scarred product of a broken, loveless home and my mother was a nominal non-practising believer whose faith had been side-tracked by marrying him.

I was sent to Sunday school as soon as I could walk by my mother and was nurtured by my aunt and uncle in the Christian faith. They were sincere loving believers to whom I am grateful for providing an environment where I could explore and question within an (albeit limited) religious framework. During these years my enquiring mind, like a sponge, absorbed by osmosis much of what formed the pillars of "truth" which would become the constructs of my consciousness.

This began my religious indoctrination and the formation of my beliefs about God. The religious programming of my mind obscured my view of who I am by misrepresenting Him in the image of G-O-D, the distant deity who occasionally made an unlikely appearance. If He did show up, the bushes were the best place to hide and cover up to appease the expected inevitable judgment to follow.

I had always believed without question that there was a God but never as a child, despite sitting through hundreds of gospel messages, did I choose to follow Him. That was until I left my comfortable local school environment at the age of 12 to attend a grammar school in another town about ten miles away. Ten miles might seem nothing to you but it was another world to me as I had only ever travelled locally and throughout my entire childhood only had one holiday, which was one night in a bed and breakfast about 100 miles away. Travelling twenty miles every day to school and back opened my eyes to a new vista but revealed people who seemed harder and more world-weary than I had been used to. What was missing from these people who seemed a little darker, less kind and more discontented than those that I was familiar with?

I questioned what the difference was, where the light was, and drew the conclusion that the missing light was God. That in itself was enough to convince me to pursue that light for myself. So alone in my bedroom in 1970 I prayed a simple prayer where I made a commitment to follow Jesus, the light. There were no real emotions, no fireworks, no flashing lights and no sounds of trumpets heralding that day, nothing that I was able to see, feel or hear. But I now know that heaven rejoiced that God's dream and desire for my destiny began another season. I simply believed and now simply I knew; and to be honest I have never doubted to this day.

I now realise that the following scriptures from the Mirror Bible are the truth of my design that was to take me on a 45-year journey to discover its reality. The truth and love of God who I now know is Father, Son and Spirit and the reality of my inheritance in sonship contained within these verses actually led me on a journey of discovery that took me from the left to the right side of my brain, from religion to relationship, from slavery and orphanhood to sonship and from earth to heaven.

He is the architect of our design; his heart dream realized our coming of age in Christ (Ephesians 1:5 MIR).

This is how we fit into God's picture: Christ is the measure of our portion, we are in him, invented and defined in him. God's blueprint intention is on exhibition in us. Everything he accomplishes is inspired by the energy and intent of his affection (Ephesians 1:11 MIR).

He engineered us from the start to fit the mold of sonship and likeness according to the exact blueprint of his design. We see the original and intended shape of our lives preserved in his Son; he is the firstborn from the same womb that reveals our genesis. He confirms that we are the invention of God (Romans 8:29 MIR).

On the journey through this book, I will attempt to be nonlinear in my approach by weaving together various threads until the tapestry is complete. I will attempt to follow the various multi-coloured threads from beginning to end to present the wondrous image of the Son which is mirrored in my own sonship. I am an example of God the great architect's design, revealed through the conversations of Father, Son and Spirit within the circle of their relationship, a relationship into which we are all now invited.

Some of the threads we will follow to create this tapestry are:

> Fatherhood and sonship
> Seeing in the spirit
> Engaging heaven
> Soul and spirit
> Unravelling theology
> Deconstructing the mind

This is not a theology book but a testimony.

I am not trying to explain or defend everything I have experienced. I am not wishing to create some new theology or doctrine from my encounters, so please try to read with an open mind. Do not be offended by what you may not understand; just let your spirit resonate with what it connects with and leave anything else for another day. My hope is that the testimony of my relationship with our heavenly Father will inspire you to pursue a deeper relationship with Him as a son (or daughter) yourself.

Beyond Slavery to Sonship

I want to share my personal journey with you of how my relationship with God as Father was restored and how He began to father me.

My journey to sonship begins with my own father. In some ways it mirrors the story of Adam and his Father God. I was to discover on my journey that God as Father has always been there longing for me to return to a walking relationship with Him. Notice I said *walking* relationship not *working* relationship. When the Father walked with His son Adam in the gardens it was for fellowship, sharing heart to heart and mind to mind. Adam walked with the Father in the garden that He had created for him and also in the Father's personal garden in the heavenlies which earth was supposed to reflect. I myself later had the joy and privilege of treading in those long forgotten footprints... but I am getting ahead of myself.

The loving Father

The Father's heart and true nature are expressed in the parable of the prodigal son (or a more accurate title would be "the loving father"). The father in the story represents our heavenly Father and is the only biblical occasion where God runs. This story would become so meaningful to me when God was revealed to me as Father, a truth which had been so obscured by the earthly relationship with my own father.

Then he said, "There was once a man who had two sons. The younger said to his father, 'Father, I want right now what's coming to me.' So the father divided the property between them. It wasn't long before the younger son packed his bags and left for a distant country. There, undisciplined and dissipated, he wasted everything he had. After he had gone through all his money, there was a bad famine all through that country and he began to hurt. He signed on with a citizen there who assigned him to his fields to slop the pigs. He was so hungry he would have eaten the corncobs in the pig slop, but no one would give him any.

"That brought him to his senses. He said, 'All those farmhands working for my father sit down to three meals a day, and here I am starving to death. I'm going back to my father. I'll say to him, Father, I've sinned against God, I've sinned before you; I don't deserve to be called your son. Take me on as a hired hand.' He got right up and went home to his father.

"When he was still a long way off, his father saw him. His heart pounding, he ran out, embraced him, and kissed him. The son started his speech: 'Father, I've sinned against God, I've sinned before you; I don't deserve to be called your son ever again.'

"But the father wasn't listening. He was calling to the servants, 'Quick. Bring a clean set of clothes and dress him. Put the family ring on his finger and sandals on his feet. Then get a grain-fed heifer and roast it. We're going to feast! We're going to have a wonderful time! My son is here – given up for dead and now alive! Given up for lost and now found!' And they began to have a wonderful time" (Luke 15:11-24 TM).

You may have had a father who was a good reflection of God to you, but most people do not. Our own upbringing often becomes the biggest obstacle and hindrance to our knowing that God is actually a father. I can honestly say that the thought never occurred to me. I was totally blinded to that truth. God was 'Jesus' or 'Lord' and that is both how I saw Him and addressed Him in the monologues which were my prayers.

God was never the Holy Spirit either but that story is another thread to follow.

My earthly father

My father was a distant man who showed very little emotion towards me. What emotions I saw him express were towards animals rather than people: animals are one of the safer options if you suffer from being rejected like he did. He was abandoned by his own father at the age of 6 and as the product of a broken home he himself never had a role model of fatherhood. That is an explanation of why he was the way he was in our non-relationship. I never blamed him or had any bitterness towards him but it still had a devastating effect on my relationship with God, my wife and family, and in fact all my relationships. He probably felt rejected and abandoned and most likely made judgments which later came upon him. From my experience of the generational issues and familiar spirits which I have had to deal with in my life, he must have had needs and emotional pain. He started with emotional and spiritual disadvantages and, because he never found a way to overcome them, therefore I did too.

I cannot remember a conversation with him of any consequence, or remember him ever telling me he loved me or showing me any physical affection. I cannot remember any verbal affirmation, encouragement or any support from him of any kind throughout my childhood. He never came to watch any of my school activities or sports or showed any real interest in me as a person. I now see how this neglect scarred and distorted my self-image and destroyed any notion of sonship. There was never any physical or verbal abuse but I was deprived emotionally which had equally serious effects that I could not see.

He was a builder by trade and a good provider for the family but to all intents and purposes he was an absent father. That absence became even more obvious when he withdrew even further into the distance of his own world as a result of the first of several affairs. Eventually he disappeared altogether when I was a teenager and the family history of divorce repeated itself. If it were not for my uncle George who was a kind, loving and godly man there would have been no glimmer of what a father could be.

Looking back, our boxer dog Bonzo was the object of my father's affection and also created in me a love for animals. I loved that dog, who was a companion from birth until he died when I was thirteen. That was the only time I ever saw my father cry. I love all animals except cats and that too has its roots in the non-relationship with my father. Later in life, when I became more aware of the negative effects that an emotionally absent father can have, I remembered a stray cat called Ricki which inserted itself into our family. I remember my father lavishing the affection I was never given on that cat and although not aware of the fact at the time I became acutely jealous of it; so much so that when I was alone in the house I would dropkick it out of the door, hoping my cruelty would drive it away. My deep inner need to be loved by a father overruled my loving nature towards animals and that outworked towards that cat. I have since asked for and received forgiveness but I still don't like cats so I guess there is still some restoration to be done.

Hope for healing

Even with God as our Father we may still feel like an orphan if our earthly father was not there for us physically or emotionally. Our past experiences will affect our present and our future if they are not dealt with and healed. The good news is that we can all be set free and restored to know our true identity as children of God, if we recognise that the God-shaped hole in us can only be filled with a relationship with God himself as a loving Father. We may have tried to fill the emptiness and pain of the rejection we have in our emotions with substitute relationships or painkillers of various description or prescription.

Some of the things the world offers us are other relationships, success, money, power, position, and work. We try to use these things to fill the hole but they often make the pain worse. We can self-medicate with many things to ease the pain and take the edge off our emptiness: alcohol, drugs, gambling, sex, pornography, exercise, food, shopping etc. These things all offer us false hope and often leave us broken, damaged, hurting, angry, rejected and addicted. We can end up feeling empty, hollow, hopeless and disillusioned with life and still not finding the answers to the questions we don't even know we are asking.

We all have our own personal stories. You may have never have known a father or mother or you may have had many substitute fathers. You may have feelings of anger, bitterness and resentment towards your parents. You may have rationalised your life and have no surface emotions. My journey was to discover that there is hope for healing, reconciliation and restoration of relationships. That hope is

Jesus the second Adam, who came to recover all that was lost by the first Adam and restores our relationship with the Father. Most of us are still in that process of learning what it is to be fathered correctly.

Substitute

My inner need drew me towards other objects which could meet my immediate need for love and affection. From an early age I tried to use relationships with women as a substitute to fill the hole in my emotions. For others it is relationships with men because they are looking for a father replacement. Those relationships with women caused more damage, hurt, pain and rejection but I needed them to fill the emptiness of my inner emotional needs.

I said 'objects' because my view of women had been perverted and distorted by the images I saw when discovering my father's stash of pornography when I was about 10 years old. I now realise that pornography creates a false image of women which becomes the object of our desire for love. All my brokenness was projected onto images which offered a temporary fix but required no intimacy or actual relationship. Pornography warped my understanding of real relationships but fuelled my need for affection and drove me to seek relationships with girls during my teenage years. Those relationships began just after my salvation aged 12, and were a constant source of guilt, shame and condemnation but none of that could overcome the drive of my inner needs. I had a number of relationships which were only a temporary solution but I always felt better about life and myself while I was in one. Many of those relationships lasted several months as I tried selfishly to maintain them. The need for love often produces damage in the form of broken hearts and I caused as well as suffered that pain. The effects of that damage would be debilitating throughout my life until I was able to deal with them, and it adversely affected my relationship with God, my wife and my children.

"Daddy, I love you"

I remember a moment in my life where I was disarmed by my one year old daughter Hannah. Hannah could talk before she could walk and she toddled up to me one day when I was sitting in my lounge watching TV, looked me right in the eyes, and said "Daddy, I love you". Determined not to be like my dad, I had told her that I loved her many times, but now I froze as if transfixed, caught in a reality which was not mine. I could not speak. I could not respond as she looked lovingly at me. I was shocked at my own reaction and this was God's provocation to admit that I needed help. Asking for help was something I rarely or ever did. I was extremely self-sufficient, independent and very capable of problem-solving but I had my own mechanisms for emotions: I mentally packaged them neatly away, filed in my mind under 'dealt with', 'forgiven and forgotten'.

You see, I did not do emotion. I was a real chip off my father's block - something I would have hated to admit. I was thick-skinned, rarely affected by anything anyone did or said, and I saw this as a real strength so I defended it. In fact it was a strong defence mechanism which had protected me from further hurt but had become a prison in which I was trapped. Eventually, in order to get at my father wounds, the layers that had been built up needed to be removed.

This experience with my daughter shocked me enough to ask for help. God used my own family to challenge me to deal with the things in my heart. Those things that had protected and guarded me had also locked me up so that I could not feel God's love. We have to overcome the obstacles in our life that will stop us from experiencing intimacy.

There were many levels of issues in me but the root was father issues. Everything was connected to my woundedness in fatherhood and sonship. My friends who were trying to minister inner healing joked that I was like a block of granite, seemingly impervious to prayer. I always had an answer that could deflect the probing questions, using some theological position to protect myself.

Breakthrough

Then I had a breakthrough. While I was being ministered to, a memory resurfaced which I had long ago buried, along with the pain associated with it. For a moment I contemplated whether or not to even go there as I knew that I had buried this one particular incident because it had caused major trauma emotionally, compounded by its foundation in my lack of a father's love.

I decided to take the risk of exposure and I was literally transported back to that day. I was back in 1975 on a Saturday in Lamorna Cove. I had travelled the 20 miles by bus to see my girlfriend of 6 months. I was in the middle of my O-level exams but I had a greater drive, so on a sunny day in June I arrived at her house. I was greeted warmly but soon was asked if I could help cut the lawn with an old hand mower. Of course I wanted to be the hero so I set about it with great gusto and after 3 hours and many blisters I had finished. Then, after lunch, came the devastating news that my girlfriend wanted to break up with me for the summer. I just broke emotionally and wept and pleaded with her for hours. I was distraught. I had never experienced anything so painfully embarrassing in my life. I was exposed and vulnerable.

My pitiful emotional manipulation caused her to relent but the damage was done, my heart was wounded and broken. On the return bus journey the fateful vow was made and the memory of it was now right in front of my eyes. I vowed never to be hurt again, and that vow became a mental walled non-emotional prison which locked me in and others out. It was a safety barrier around my heart protecting me from hurt and damage but keeping everyone else at arm's distance. I thought it was a strength to be thick-skinned and impervious to hurt. I became a very logical and analytical person, using my intellect to package things up so I didn't have to deal with the emotions.

Soon afterwards she broke up with me anyway, but I didn't care and spent the whole summer demonstrating my new-found "freedom" in a number of holiday romances that did nothing but cover my denial of pain.

In that ministry time I renounced that vow and chose to forgive her and release her from the debt that was outstanding against her and woven into the fabric of my emotions. My whole life and all my relationships, including my relationship with God, had been negatively affected from that point on. I was locked into that fateful day but now something broke open with dramatic effects. All those negative emotions for so long imprisoned began to pour out, to the delight of my wife who had been longing for that day, because these issues had had a significantly negative effect on my marriage during those early years. I am so grateful to my loving wife Deb, who although damaged by my protection mechanisms and my

23

inability to share emotionally, stuck with me and is a wonderful wife and mother, often compensating for my many failures.

Eventually equilibrium was restored and I was able to feel and express healthy emotions. I was still on a journey of restoration to be able to love and receive love again but a layer separating me from the Father was removed.

Revealed as Father

Over the years, God met with me in various encounters which He used to heal my heart. I struggled with the concept, as so many of us do because of our own fathers, but He broke through that and put His arms around me. I never thought of God as Father; it was not just that it never computed or made sense but that mostly it never even occurred to me that God was a father. I had read the Bible many times and must have read all the scriptures describing God as Father but they were completely invisible to me.

The first time God managed to reveal Himself to me as Father was in 1990 when I was worshipping in a small group of people. My spirit was open and my guard down when I sensed God speaking to me, as a thought in my mind. He said "I am your Father". I then had my first physical encounter when I felt His arms, and I felt His presence, and it enabled me to begin to talk to Him and to communicate with Him as Father. That was also my first encounter with an angel but I will leave that to another thread.

My eyes were open and now I could begin to see and feel all that I had been blinded to. This was not a quick fix by the waving of a magic wand: I still had many deep-rooted issues surrounding my own father to deal with.

The root issue was my father wound but the surface issues were around my rejection. I started to receive help to deal with my emotional damage. A lot of hidden emotions which I had buried came to the surface, and most were negative to begin with. I felt attacked and vulnerable. I became defensive at times. My emotions began to open up and that led to the deeper issue of not being fathered becoming uncovered.

The main issues started to bubble up to the surface of my broken heart. Fortunately I learned the ministry tools that enabled me to forgive and release and become free. God started to break in on my life in a more intense way in 1993 when we were involved in a move of God that was very similar to what was to take place in Toronto the following year. There were powerful demonstrations of God's love unveiling the Father's heart for His children but manifesting in some very weird experiences, including episodes of intense uncontrollable laughter and strange occurrences of being stuck, unable to move. Whatever God was doing it opened my heart and revealed the depth of my father wound issues.

I made an 'invoice' that catalogued all the areas in which the lack of a father's love and affirmation had negatively affected my life and then began the process of forgiving and releasing my dad for all that I was owed. I struggled to connect emotionally and was doing it by choice and will. It was a picture of a picture that changed everything: during an inner healing session I saw a picture of a framed photograph that used to be in our house when I was a child. It was a black and white picture of me sitting on my father's knee when I was about 2 years old, wearing a knitted jumper, shorts and a bow tie. It suddenly hit me that this was a pose for a photograph of something that never occurred in real life. It was a sham of a picture that represented the sham of our relationship and the full weight of the emotions hit me. I was angry and sad and disappointed all rolled into one ball of emotion which I felt intensely. I was able to forgive and release my dad for the sham of the relationship and really mean it. As a result I was even able to visit him and tell him that I forgave him. I told him I loved him, and hugged him. Just as I had done with Hannah, he froze and could not respond, but I was on a journey to freedom and restoration. There was restoration from my side and I was able to introduce my children to their grandfather shortly before he died.

The experience sparked by the memory of that sham photograph was intense but I still did not release the emotions I felt as I just did not know how. As a result of prophetic words, God called us to leave the town of our birth and move to Barnstaple in North Devon to plant 'Freedom Fellowship - Church on the Move'. The church was birthed in the same move of the Spirit during a series of meetings early in 1994 called "More for 94" almost simultaneous with the Toronto outpouring at the Airport Vineyard.

I travelled the 110 miles to Barnstaple each Wednesday for 4 months to lay the biblical foundations of the church. During one of those sessions we were worshipping when surreally I found myself flat out on the floor weeping and wailing uncontrollably. All the pent-up emotions and pain that had been exposed during the ministry relating to my father wounds came flooding out like a torrent of sorrow, grief and pain. For 45 minutes God opened the floodgates. Those around me were nonplussed but fortunately just left me until all the pain came out and God's healing love came flooding in. God turned off the tap and I got up feeling 100 pounds lighter emotionally and delivered the evening's teaching as if nothing at happened.

We moved the family from St. Ives up to Barnstaple in August 1994. I continued to work in the hospital biochemistry laboratory in Truro until November 1994, commuting the 110 miles twice a week. We began public meetings in the autumn of 1994 with praise and worship being the key focus of our gatherings. During one of those gatherings in 1996, Mike Collins, our saxophonist at the time, played a long note that began soaring; and supernaturally I went soaring too, into a heavenly vision. This was what I now realise was my first encounter in heaven. The Father picked me up and bounced me on His knee and gave me a revelation of my value and worth, finally removing the sham of my earthly father's relationship with me. This continued for 45 minutes in earthly time where I was lost in complete bliss, totally unaware of anything going on around but absorbed in the mystic union of my Father's love. This amazing love encounter restored me to sonship but all the inner healing and restoration had only brought me from minus 100 to zero on the fatherhood scale. I still needed to be fathered.

My relationship with God as Father continued to develop over the years and I felt healed and restored to the degree that I knew, but I was to discover how much more there was beyond what I could ever have imagined or thought.

In 2009 I was attending our Sunday morning gathering where we were having a visiting speaker. During the worship time I started to feel very uncomfortable and physically sick in the pit of my stomach. I knew this was a spiritual attack right at the heart of my fatherhood. Accusations began to fill my mind, overwhelming me with guilt and condemnation about how bad I was as a father. I acutely felt the pain of how my many failings had affected my four children. Some friends noticed I was obviously struggling and began to pray for me prophesying God's love and forgiveness. I was physically sick and totally wiped out. God spoke directly to my heart, calling things that are not as if they are, telling me that I was a good father. I felt anything but, as I knew that my brokenness and inadequateness had caused them pain but those words of affirmation began a process of restoration.

I went home to bed but knew I had to speak to the children and explain. Even now I don't really know what I said but something broke and a door through which the enemy had access was closed. Now my relationship with all of them and with my grandchildren, although not perfect (from my perspective at least), is better than it has ever been.

In May 2010 I received a prophetic word by letter from my good friend Mike Bryant which included the invitation to ascend. A few days later I went to a conference about 75 miles away with Stacey Campbell and Ryan Wyatt, intending to just attend for one day. On the drive down God spoke to me and said "This time is just for you and me. Don't minister or focus on receiving ministry, just give me this time." I thought I was going to appear really rude but decided to go for it, without any idea of what was going to happen. From the first note of the worship time, with songs I did not even know but seemed to all be about love, my heart melted and I became desperate for more. I was consumed by love and fell in love with God like 'first love' was always meant to be. I had to find some accommodation and stay on for the full three days so that I could just keep immersed and baptised in love. When finally I drove home, cocooned in a bubble of God's love, the Father asked if I would spend forty days with Him on a fast. Without hesitation I said yes and began the pursuit of the invitation to ascend into heaven.

I will go into the details of that fast on another thread but after nineteen days I went into a trance and spent the next three weeks in the heavenly realms. During those amazing face to face encounters with Jesus and the Holy Spirit, deep down I knew that I had not engaged the Father. I did not know whether I was avoiding Him or He was avoiding me but something was gnawing at me. Eventually as I was sitting talking with Jesus, He said "you have a father wound" I began to protest that I had forgiven and released my father, but I did not get very far before I looked deeply into His eyes and my defences dissolved. I looked down and saw a scar about 14 inches long over my heart. The scar tissue of my father wounds was still evident to the loving discernment of His eyes. He said "Do you want to be healed?"

The instant I thought "yes", the Father walked up to me and looked at me with those eyes and just said "I love you, I love you" over and over, each statement slowly removing the scar tissue. For 45 minutes in earth time He continued to pour out His love, restoring, reconciling and redeeming my pain and brokenness. So began some wonderful adventures.

Intimacy

I started to engage God, who is Father Son and Spirit, within my spirit where they reside in the kingdom:

For remember, the kingdom of God is within you (Luke 17:21b MEV).

Ian Clayton, a forerunner and explorer of the heavenly order of Melchizedek of which we are all called to be part, was given a scroll in heaven that contained a diagrammatic representation of our three-part being: spirit, soul and body.

Now may the God of peace Himself sanctify you entirely; and may your spirit and soul and body be preserved complete, without blame at the coming of our Lord Jesus Christ (1 Thessalonians 5:23)

I discovered we have a First Love Gate within our spirit that connects to the kingdom of God's rule and reign within us and is a portal or wormhole to Eden. This is the door which Jesus refers to in the book of Revelation:

Behold, I stand at the door and knock; if anyone hears My voice and opens the door, I will come in to him and will dine with him, and he with Me (Revelation 3:20).

Most of us may never have heard Jesus knocking or realised that there is a real and literal spiritual dimension within us and therefore have never opened this gate. The result is that we only have a trickle of the River of Life which is behind that gate as it flows under the threshold, as described in Ezekiel 47:1.

We can drink from that spring, the source of the Holy Spirit's life, which Jesus talks about in John 4:14, but unless we open up the door it never becomes the rivers of living water promised in John 7:37-38. That amazing trickle of life enables us to have the fruit of the Spirit and the gifts of the Spirit functioning in our lives but it is nothing compared to the torrent that could flow from the heavenly source of the Tree and River of Life, Jesus, who is life itself. If only we would hear Him knocking and open the First Love Gate and then all the gateways of our spirit, soul and body, then that heavenly river could flow through our lives and we would become a gateway of heaven into the earth.

I used to think of intimacy as the warm fuzzy feelings which people expressed when they described their experiences with God but that was because I was comparing myself with others. One day the Father spoke to me and asked "How do you feel my love"?

Me: "What do You mean?"

God: "When do you feel the most loved?"

Me: "When we spend time with each other, when You talk to me, when You share things with me."

I read a book many years ago about languages of love in relation to marriage but the concept is equally applicable to our relationship with God. The love languages are: physical affection, quality time, words of affirmation, gifts and acts of service. Quality time is my heavenly love language; it fills my emotional tank. For me, quality time with the Father sometimes means just hanging out with each other without even talking but at other times it is where He shares revelation of His heart with me. The Father spending time with me does it for me and makes me feel special and loved.

God communicates to me in so many different ways: through books, films, the Bible, visions, impressions, concepts and ideas. But He also speaks to me directly in conversation during which I tend to spend more time listening than talking. When I do ask questions He always answers in His own way;

sometimes with more questions, but He always lets me know exactly what I need to know. Heart to heart relationship is what really floats my boat.

He relates to me according to my redemptive gift, which is prophet/teacher. I am unique, special just like you, and He fathers me uniquely, according to my destiny. He will do that for you too if you let Him.

I never really took much notice of the construct of my spirit. As soon as I opened that First Love Gate I was just totally captivated with the love and light that exploded from that gateway. I was often surrounded by the embrace of Father, Son and Spirit and held in a heavenly hug. When I began to teach this to others, God took the opportunity to take me deeper into the revelation of His love. My habit had been to drink that living water of the Spirit, take the yoke of Jesus and abdicate the throne of my life (the seat of rest and government) to the Father. Then I would move on to whatever I was called to do that day from the perspective of responsibility in sonship. What God taught me was that all heavenly and earthly governmental responsibility must flow from the intimacy of the relationship of sonship. Our level of heavenly government is proportional to the depth of relationship. I can't be a son without a father and my level of relationship with my Father was far less than He desired.

For months, whenever I opened that gate I was held within the Father's embrace in a cardiognostic heart to heart encounter where I was taken deeper and deeper into His love and therefore into my identity as a son.

God communicated to me through various living words. I felt them more than heard them: they just filled my being with overwhelming truth. Truth of the very precepts, nature and character of the Father was like an intense light that flooded into my being at a level beyond my cognitive ability to know and understand. My spirit resonated with that revelation and the words were living and active just as explained in Hebrews 4:12. Here are some of the living words that illuminated my reality:

Father - my creator, my sustainer, my essence, my rest, my shalom, my affirmer, my accepter, my peace, my love, my provider, my protector, my healer, my sanctifier, my righteousness, my banner, my victory, my security, my identity, my anchor, my hope, my delight, my purpose, my glorifier, my rock, my restorer.

Father - my reconciler, my transformer, my transfigurer, my renewer, my conformer, my forgiver, my strength, my authority, my power, my eternal destination, my eternal home, my reference point.

I began to walk with the Father through the realms of heaven, enjoying many wondrous and joyous Garden of Eden encounters.

Gardens

On one occasion I found myself sitting on a swing with a small bench-like seat which was hanging from the branch of a tree on a small area of grass. The Father was gently pushing me on the swing so I assumed we were somewhere in a heavenly garden. I asked Him where we were and He told me we were in the garden of my heart. I was somewhat surprised as I did not know I had a garden or that it was even possible to be consciously aware of my heart. Of course our heart is within our soul which is a spiritual construct not bound by physical space. He told me that the garden was an inner representation of the physical garden that God gave Adam to tend and cultivate.

Over time the Father showed me how to tend and cultivate the garden of my heart by planting seeds of testimonies by the river of life that flows there so that they produced fruitful trees. He taught me to release the creativity of sonship to see my garden grow and expand. What began as an untended wasteland is now a beautifully cultivated garden where I can continually eat the fruit that grows there.

I often spent hours laying in the green pasture by the still and quiet waters enjoying fellowship with the Father or Jesus the Good Shepherd. I learned to be still and know God as Father, Son and Spirit in the intimacy of my secret place. Psalm 23 is a wonderful description of this intimate place where my soul can be restored and become fruitful. I learned to eat the fruit of my testimonies so it became a doorway to re-engage past encounters or give the fruit of my testimonies to others.

I learned to follow the river of life flowing in my garden back to its heavenly source in Eden, God's garden. That garden overflowing with abundant life, joy and peace became a place of exploration and adventure. Everything from the river of life to the cascading waterfalls - where deep calls to deep - is alive with vibrant living colours and fragrances; where emotions are released and fill the glorious atmosphere beyond any earthly description.

I learned that I could ascend the waterfalls (the physics of heaven defies the laws of the natural realm; as Neo discovered in *The Matrix*, bending the spoon is much easier once you realise there is no spoon!). Then I followed the river by way of a path that meandered through beautiful multi-coloured vegetation beyond description until I eventually discovered the throne of grace and the judgment seat, which I will explain more about later. Following my first encounter with the judgment seat, the Spirit of the Fear of the Lord led me to a waterfall which gave me access to the Father's garden for the first time.

On one occasion I was there and I was floating, not touching anything, almost part of the atmosphere. I was feeling at one with the Father, intimate and loved; and I just exploded. Every atom of me dispersed out into the whole of creation and I felt what it was like to be one with it.

This experience awoke my desire for sonship; it still has an incredibly powerful effect on my life. That encounter stirred the desire in me to answer the groan of creation as a son and see it restored back into harmony as it was originally intended. I felt what it was like to be in harmony with everything and also had this distant memory of what everything was like when it was still in perfect harmony with God.

Those experiences have a deep meaning to me and inspired many of my later choices to respond to God-given opportunities. My perspective of everything changed and now I see a bigger picture, the restoration of all things.

On another occasion, following the River of Life led me to a bridge where Jesus was calmly waiting. He looked knowingly into my eyes and gently beckoned me to cast all my burdens onto His broad shoulders. "You can't carry those things into the Father's garden." I happily complied, not that I felt particularly burdened but I assumed He knew best. I actually felt naked as I walked across the bridge and followed some steps into the Father's garden, into an atmosphere of supreme peace. There were amazingly beautiful plants issuing fragrances of peace and rest. I could not see the Father but sensed and felt His presence. The atmosphere was thick, tangible, filled with peace such that I just relaxed, leaning back until I was floating in pure unadulterated rest. I started to gently rock as I pondered but immediately felt the Father's thoughts penetrate my mind, "No activity here!" So I stopped thinking and sank even deeper into rest. It just felt like I was communing with the Father's heart, 'being still and knowing' (Psalm 46:10).

That is all I did the first few times I was drawn back to that atmosphere but then one day as I walked across the bridge the Father was there to meet me. He beckoned me rather than spoke and we walked to a pool of the deepest blue, fed by the river, into which a waterfall was cascading almost gently as if in slow motion. I just knew that this pool held unknown expectations that drew me to dive in and swim down deeper and deeper until in the sparkling water I saw floating a treasure chest. I opened the lid to discover a host of golden coins. I was drawn to take one and eat it; there are many things that it seems just right to eat, including scrolls and gems. As it entered me it exploded with life and a thought of the Father filled my mind. I was later to discover that each of these coins represents one of the vast sum of thoughts the Father has about us as individuals.

How precious also are Your thoughts to me, O God! How vast is the sum of them! (Psalm 139:17 NASB)

Your thoughts and plans are treasures to me, O God! I cherish each and every one of them! How grand in scope! How many in number! (Psalm 139:17 VOI).

That thought was exactly what I needed to hear but it was more than just hearing; it exploded into my consciousness and I 'knew that I knew' it as truth. It was a truth that revolutionised an area where I was struggling to believe the reality about myself and what was possible.

I was in the Father's garden on another occasion when I felt drawn back to the pool of God's thoughts but as I swam down I was caught in a whirlpool that took me past the chest and through a vortex. I suddenly found myself in what I now know is the Father's heart outside of time and space. I was back in the creative womb of His desire that birthed my existence. I stood in the midst of love's creative power and I felt I was home and lost all at once. My mind was completely undone but my spirit was connected to my eternal identity as a son in the midst of the Father's love, connected to what was before there was anything but the circle of relationship of Father, Son and Spirit. I was in the midst of the conversation that formed the thoughts of my existence. This amazing place, unfathomable with my mind, became a place where 'what was' would be the source that informed 'what is' to release 'what will be'.

Here, cocooned in love, I heard the Father say "Let me show you My mind." Instantly I was in the midst of the great conversation that framed my destiny and I heard my name whispered within that conversation of the ages. Then the Father unveiled something which expanded my conscious reality: He showed me in a glimpse how He is connected to everyone who has ever lived and who ever will live (by current estimates, around 108 billion people and counting). He is connected to all time and space, every microsecond, with every choice, and He is so overflowing with extravagant, lavish abundance that He desires and gives opportunity to bring good out of every choice, even the most stupid and inane ones. This experience took me beyond love as an emotion to the core essence of who God is. It changed how I saw the world and everyone in it.

People get to heavenly places in a variety of ways and have different heavenly experiences. I found pools, rivers and waterfalls which all led me to places that were beyond anything I could ever have imagined. Other people find different ways because God relates to us in a fashion that we can understand. Heaven is very individual for different people, which is why I try not to describe it in too much detail. Everyone needs to experience these things in their own way, having their own personal encounters which are real for them.

I saw my earthly father again more recently. I was speaking at a conference in Phoenix in 2016. Whilst facilitating an activation relating to God as Father I found myself in the Court of the Upright in the heavenly realms. A figure came from amongst the cloud of witnesses and walked up to me. It was my earthly father. We embraced and he told me that he was proud of me. I felt his love and an overwhelming sense of joy as a circle had been completed. I think of these types of experiences as little kisses of blessing from God.

Included in the circle of relationship

John 14 is my favourite chapter in the Bible. Let the truth of your inclusion with the circle of relationship and the Father's heart come to life as you read it in the Mirror Bible translation:

Set your troubled hearts at ease by letting your belief conclude in God as you rest your confidence in me. What makes my Father's house home, is your place in it! If this was not the ultimate conclusion of my mission why would I even bother to do what I am about to do if it was not to prepare a place for you? I have come to persuade you of a place of seamless union where you belong. The proportions of what I will accomplish are astonishing! I will prepare a highway for you, just as in the Oriental custom, where people would go before a king to level the roads to make it possible for royalty to journey with ease and comfort. By fully identifying myself with you I would fully identify you with me so that you may be completely at home where I am! (John 14:1-3 MIR).

Jesus said, "My I am-ness [mirrored in you] is your way; this is your truth and also your life! Every single person can now come face to face with the Father entirely because of my doing" (John 14:6 MIR).

Are you not convinced that I am in the Father and that the Father is in me? We are in seamless union. The words that I speak to you are not my independent opinion or ideas; the Father in me addresses you; this conversation then translates into the Father's action unveiled in my doing (John 14:10 MIR)

In that day you will know that just as I am in my Father, you are in me and I am in you! (Now picture 4 circles with the one fitting into the other - The outer circle is the Father, then Jesus in the Father, then us in Jesus, and the Spirit in us! This spells inseparable, intimate oneness! Note that it is not our knowing that positions Jesus in the Father or us in them! Our knowing simply awakens us to the reality of our redeemed union! Gold does not become gold when it is discovered but it certainly becomes currency!)

Whoever resonates and treasures the completeness of my prophetic purpose cannot but fall in love with me and also find themselves to be fully participating in my Father's love and I will love this one and make myself distinctly known and real to each one individually. In this embrace of inseparable union love rules! (John 14:20-21 MIR)

The original life of the Father revealed in his son is the life the Spirit now conducts within us. Slavery is such a poor substitute for sonship! They are opposites; the one leads forcefully through fear while sonship responds fondly to Abba Father. His Spirit resonates within our spirit to confirm the fact that we originate in God. Because we are his offspring, we qualify to be heirs; God himself is our portion, we co-inherit with Christ. Since we were represented and included in his suffering we equally participate in the glory of his resurrection (Romans 8:14-17).

Beyond Hearing and Seeing to Living and Knowing in the Spirit.

I have been on this journey for many years without even realising it. I think of myself as a normal sort of guy. I am not known to be flaky; or at least, no-one has thought so until recently! I like sports and movies, especially science fiction, and cruise holidays (or vacations, for our cousins across the pond). The supernatural lifestyle is about being real and not being super-spiritual. It is us being real people, but real people who are the sons of God, called to demonstrate the Kingdom of God on the earth as it is in heaven. The sons of God are beyond just human beings: we are living beings who are being transfigured or metamorphosed into godlike beings. For this transformation to take place we have to learn to live in the spirit realms as spirit beings.

Born from above

A little more about my background will set the scene for this thread. As I shared in the previous thread, I had no real Christian heritage in my family. My mum is a Christian, and she did send me to Sunday school, but she wasn't really actively practising her faith when I was growing up. When, in 1970, I made a personal commitment in my own bedroom, I did not really feel anything. It was just that I decided to follow God, though at that time it was little more than 'fire insurance'.

Years later, when I eventually engaged in heaven, and I was in the record room within the Court of Scribes looking for my destiny scroll, I went to my birth date and I didn't find it. Much to my consternation, there was no scroll there. An angel told me, "You need to look in a different place. You need to look when you first came to the realisation of being born from above." But I didn't know exactly when that was. I knew it was sometime in 1970, but I had no idea what date it was. So I remember saying to the angel, "That's not fair." He took me to the right place and it was then that I discovered the date was the 18th of September 1970, because that's where the scroll was in the record. So I found out when I discovered I was born again, which was really fun.

I had always believed in God and I never doubted anything, but it wasn't what I would call the most dynamic of relationships. I did, though, have a very keen interest in the Bible, and I studied it a lot because it was in my nature to be inquisitive, always wanting to find things out. At that time in my life I didn't have any experience or any real emotions in my relationship with Him.

I have discovered over the years that God, who is Father, Son and Spirit, has a real sense of humour – and often exercises it at my expense. If I were God I would not have chosen me; but of course God chooses the foolish things of the world to confound the wise. I guess I would rather be a fool for Christ than for myself but that would be another thread in its own right.

I have had to persevere and overcome what appear from my perspective to be many significant disadvantages in order to come to the place of rest I am now living in.

Public speaking

You might find this hard to believe now, but when I was a child I had a really strong fear of public speaking to such an extent that even reading aloud in school class would send me into a panic. Seriously, I would use any excuse to try to get out of the room when it came to reading or any public performance. God had other ideas so when I was a teenager I found that people kept asking me to speak. I kept saying, "You must be mad, I don't speak publicly". God didn't give up and kept inspiring people to keep asking me until one day I heard "yes" coming out of my mouth. When I heard that horrific word it just broke that whole fear of speaking and everything changed. Eventually, I realised that it was God calling me to speak on His behalf as an oracle or prophetic voice but it took many years for me to be comfortable in my own skin and accept the redemptive gifts and calls attached to my destiny.

I later discovered when I developed more insight into my brokenness that my fear originated in a traumatic event in my childhood that I had completely forgotten. I was perhaps three years old and about to perform my piece in the Sunday School anniversary before the whole Methodist church, including my mother. I suddenly stood up before my turn and cried out with a loud voice "I need a pee" at which point my red-faced highly embarrassed mother raced up the aisle from the back of the building to the choir gallery and pulled me out. Suffice it to say that was my first and last anniversary performance but it left me emotionally scarred. The enemy - our adversary - is keen to take advantage of any trauma, however small, to rob us of our destiny.

Baptisms

I came from a Methodist background; it was a good bible-believing chapel and I progressed to teaching Sunday school in my late teenage years. I eventually became more spiritually discerning and increasingly disturbed by the more liberal way the Methodist church seemed to be heading. I began looking for an alternative, which was not easy as West Cornwall was a hotbed of Methodism. There were many brands of Methodism; Wesleyan, Primitive and Bible Christian plus several others, a Congregational Church, Salvation Army and two Anglican churches. None of them presented as a viable option.

Then in March 1975, I saw this apparition of beauty walking up the road past where I was waiting to go and play in a football match. I later discovered that she was watching the match and I began a convoluted pursuit of the girl who would later become my wife. Her family were members of one of three local Brethren assemblies which I did not even know existed. So I jumped out of the frying pan into the fire so to speak, not from any deep spiritual motive but an entirely fleshly one. Fortunately, God even weaves our brokenness into the great tapestry of His design.

A little Brethren Gospel Hall was not an ideal environment when it came to the things of the Spirit. In fact, I lived in a town where there was no Baptist Church and no one that I knew taught baptism in water, let alone the baptism in the Holy Spirit. When I read in the Bible about baptism I knew I needed to be baptised. I did not have a great understanding of what baptism really meant but I just wanted to be obedient. I had to travel twelve miles up the road to find someone who would baptise me. I was the only person I knew that got baptised in our whole town yet within three years we had a baptistry in our church. So I guess I have always been a forerunner. I had no idea that's what I was; I just followed what I discovered through my love of the scriptures.

I did not even read a whole book until I was 12 (it was H.G. Wells' *The Time Machine*) but God used books throughout my life to open my heart up to new revelation as I had no idea how to hear Him speaking to me directly. The first Christian book that really impacted me was *The Normal Christian Life* by Watchman Nee. I was sixteen and struggling with the usual guilt shame and condemnation cycle of sin and repentance (repenance) for sin. The revelation of the nature of the soul and how it should be normal to live free from the power of sin empowered me.

By accident, I came across the book *Nine O'clock in the Morning* by Dennis and Rita Bennett in 1982. As I read it, I was absolutely captivated and fascinated by the story. This was way out of my comfort zone but my spirit was resonating and leaping within me. This began a search for truth and I found a well-respected Bible teacher, Martyn Lloyd-Jones, whose book *Baptism in the Holy Spirit* now theologically convinced me that the baptism of the Holy Spirit was for today and for me.

I knew no one who had had this experience at the time so it still took me another three years to get baptised in the Spirit. I tried every ridiculous thing that the plethora of books suggested I do to trigger speaking in tongues. I said banana backwards and rubbed my lips up and down; yes I know how silly that sounds but I was desperate. I have always been rather tenacious. When I see something, and I want it, then I am willing to do whatever it takes to get it.

In the end, I said to God, "I am not asking You ever again. I have asked You for three years and if You don't want to do it then okay, fine, I'm not going to ask You again." It's not that I gave up, I just thought, "If You want to do it, You are going to have to do it". So that was it.

Within two days, a friend from my childhood reappeared in my life. He had been in the Royal Air Force and was now married and a Christian (I would never have seen that coming) but more importantly was baptised in the Holy Spirit. That gave me renewed hope and I even started teaching the youth group I was running that truth. Some of those kids began speaking in tongues - how unfair!

Then one night at a small group meeting we were worshipping and my friend put his hand on me and I got baptised in the Spirit. It was like liquid love was poured into my life. I heard the word 'revival' echo in my mind even though I didn't know what that meant. I went home, fell on my knees filled to overflowing with joy, and began with a few words of tongues. Of course, the adversary came with doubts but this experience transformed my life and I knew it was real. I became more sensitive to the Spirit's leading and my desire for God and worship just exploded. This also opened my life emotionally to God and others.

This happened while I was still in the Brethren assembly and it caused much consternation because they obviously did not believe in that sort of thing at all. We used to have open meetings in which anyone could get up and speak, so one Sunday evening I got up and gave my testimony of how I got baptised in the Holy Spirit. You could have heard a pin drop but as I was going out, one old guy in his eighties shook my hand and said, "Thank you, my boy, don't give up. I experienced that many years ago too." He was the exception. And eventually, God called me to draw people together and begin sharing my testimony with others. I began meeting in small home groups with other like-minded people, seeking and exploring together.

Supernatural

This was where I had my first encounter with a vision. It was in 1990 and I was in a small meeting of about 15 people. We were just worshipping God. I was standing, worshipping God with my eyes closed. I had a vision of an egg sandwich that just appeared right in front of me. I opened my eyes and it was still there. So I was eyeing up this egg sandwich and looking around thinking, "Is anyone else seeing this?" It was as if God said, "Eat it." You need to know, I really hate eggs. And I hate egg sandwiches. It didn't even have any ketchup on it. If it had ketchup on it, maybe it would have been okay. It was just an egg sandwich. There was no explanation, just "Eat it."

So I did. I was just really hoping no one was watching because I took it and I actually ate it. I tasted it, and it was horrible, but I did it. Then when I had finished another one appeared. "Eat this one." So, at that point, okay, 'in for a penny, in for a pound', as we say, and I ate that one as well. Immediately the power of God just fell on me. Literally, I felt electrified. I had never felt anything like that before. When I had got baptised in the Spirit I had felt love, a sort of lovely warm, fluffy feeling, but this was just like power. It was like I was plugged into the electricity socket.

Within two minutes the whole room was flattened. I was like a kid in a candy store. People were just falling on the floor; I had never seen anything like it. It was not as if I had ever experienced or really even heard of anything like that. Then I started prophesying over all those people. So egg sandwiches have never been quite the same since.

I eventually helped plant a charismatic church which was where I began to discover the more overt supernatural aspects and experiences of being a Christian. It was during one of those supernatural experiences in 1993 that I had a vision of climbing a mountain. I remember I was flat on the floor, but in the Spirit I was climbing a mountain. I climbed up the mountain and I stopped at various points on the way up. I looked out and I could see amazing things, but I could not remember any of what I saw because I did not have a reference or a grid for it then. 22 years later, God took me back and showed me all the things that I had seen in the Spirit that I could not remember. It was all the stepping stones in my testimony of this journey.

I saw many things back then but because I could not contain them I had no conscious memory of them. Yet my spirit received the revelation, and recognised those things on my journey and resonated with them (even though I didn't know what 'resonated' meant in those days).

Even before I became a Christian, I had always felt a destiny. I could not be satisfied with where I was. There was always something in me that caused me to want something more. I went on to become a scientist. I worked as a biochemist in a hospital for 18 years, all very logical, very intellect-centred, very left-brained, non-creative, and reason-based. I still had a hunger and desire for something because, as I have explained before, like Bono I still hadn't found what I was looking for.

I searched for it, for years and years. I knew there had to be more. I knew when I read the Bible that I hadn't even experienced most of what was in it, let alone anything else. I knew there must be something more than this. It was not really until I engaged in heaven that I found it. I had come home and I finally found what I had been seeking for so long.

The journey

This journey for me has been one of increasing intimacy. I have known God a long time, but known Him intimately only a very short time. I knew a lot about Him (at least, I thought I did), but knew very little of Him in terms of personal experience, even though by now I had been a Christian for years.

It has been a journey that began with word and theory but has become a continuing series of experiential encounters. When I look back on my testimony, I find that I have actually been having experiential encounters over many years; I just did not recognise them.

It has been a journey from the left side to the right side of the brain. From being very, very, left-brained I have instead become mostly right-brained. To be left-brained is to be very logical and analytical. Right-brained is very creative. We are encouraged in our educational system to be very left-brained, and in my case I went on to train and work as a scientist, which only encouraged that further. Being left-brained does not help when we come to engage in the spirit because the spirit operates very much on the right side of our brain. For example, when you pray in tongues - a spiritual activity - research has found that it is the right side of your brain that becomes active, whereas normal language operates on the left side of the brain. I had to train my brain to think and act differently.

It is a journey from earth to heaven. I used to think I would only go to heaven when I die. I had the same covenant with death that most Christians have, thinking the only time I am really going to see God is when I die.

It has been a journey from being totally earthbound to being able to engage in totally different spiritual realms and dimensions beyond anything I could have imagined or thought.

There have been so many stepping stones on this journey; it did not happen instantly. All of us are of course on our own journey: many people have had all kinds of different encounters in their lives. The difference is that God wants us to be able to have these encounters all the time, as a lifestyle, rather than on extraordinary occasions.

It has been a journey from head knowledge to heart experience. I studied a lot and knew a lot about the Bible, from a position of study and producing some really good sermons from it, but now I have experience of it, a living experience.

My journey has been from knowing something about God to knowing Him face to face and talking to Him, which is something I did not think I could do. From my religious upbringing, I thought you could not have a face to face encounter until you die - something that I found is happily not true, as otherwise I would not have been able to write and share my experiences.

It is a journey from doing things for God to doing things with Him. I was a really good steward for many years. I used to do what I felt God asked me to do, but now I have discovered that it is much better, and much more fun, to do things with Him.

It is a journey from slavery to sonship. That is a journey that huge numbers of people within the body of Christ are starting to be drawn by God to undertake. We come out of Egypt (representing the world), but Egypt does not just automatically come out of us. God wants us to come into sonship, which is a totally different way of thinking and acting, a different experience altogether. My journey has taken me from the wilderness of religious experience to the inheritance of the Promised Land; from being a good steward to being a trusted son. It has taken me many years to get there. It is a blessing that there are many forerunners who open up a way for others to cross over the "Jordan". So if you are willing to pursue your own path it will not have to take as long or be as hard as it was for those who have gone before us.

Of course, Jesus himself is the greatest forerunner of them all. He has not just gone before but He has opened up the way for all of us to cross over beyond the veil into sonship:

This hope we have as an anchor of the soul, a hope both sure and steadfast and one which enters within the veil, where Jesus has entered as a forerunner for us, having become a high priest forever according to the order of Melchizedek (Hebrews 6:19-20 NASB).

Our hearts and minds are certain; anchored securely within the innermost courts of God's immediate Presence; beyond the (prophetic) veil. By going there on our behalf, Jesus pioneered a place for us and removed every type of obstruction that could possibly distance us from the promise. In him we are represented for all time; he became our High Priest after the order of Melchizedek. We now enjoy the same privileged access he has. (He said, "I go to prepare a place for you so that you may be where I am. On that day you will no longer doubt that I and the Father are one; you will know that I am in the Father and you in me and I in you!" [John 10:30, 14:3, 20]) (Hebrews 6:19-20 MIR).

Therefore, brethren, since we have the confidence to enter the holy place by the blood of Jesus, by a new and living way which He inaugurated for us through the veil, that is, His flesh, and since we have a great priest over the house of God, let us draw near with a sincere heart in full assurance of faith... (Hebrews 10:19-22 NASB).

Brethren, this means that through what the blood of Jesus communicates and represents, we are now welcome to access this ultimate place of sacred encounter with unashamed confidence. A brand new way of life has been introduced. Because of his flesh torn on the cross (our own flesh can no longer be a valid excuse to interrupt the expression of the life of our design). We have a High Priest in the house! We are free to approach him with absolute confidence, fully persuaded in our hearts that nothing can any longer separate us from him. We are invited to draw near now! ... (Hebrews 10:19-22 MIR).

It is a journey from where we were continually asking God to come down from heaven, to where we hear and accept His continual invitation to "Come up here", going to heaven and then bringing heaven back to earth. So much of what we have done in the past has been "God, come down" or "Come, Holy Spirit". Now I realise when I look back at all the times I said "Come, Holy Spirit" that mostly what I experienced was angels engaging us.

Nowadays I never ask the Holy Spirit to come, or command Him to come, because He is God (I say 'He', but Ruach (breath, spirit) is a feminine gender word in Hebrew, and sometimes the Holy Spirit may appear feminine to you. It is not that God is male or female but that He has all the attributes that made us, both male and female, in His image).

I wonder what He thinks, all those people telling Him to come here and come there. He is very gracious and does come to meet with us in many different ways. What He really wants is for us to go and meet with Him, and in meeting with Him, to come back into this realm bringing what we have from there to here; to be a gateway of heaven on earth.

My journey is from seeing God's works to knowing His ways. These are two totally different experiences. Many of us have seen things that God has done, miracles and signs and wonders. We have had experiences with the presence of God, but God wants us to know Him; not just to have the experience of seeing what He does, but to actually know Him in person.

In all that I am sharing in this testimony, I do not want you to chase the experience, but to pursue a person and a relationship with that person. That is what God really wants. All the experiences are really just by-products. You can have an intimate relationship with God without those things, and most of the time you don't have them. I talk to people a lot about ecstatic experiences, getting whacked in the Spirit, and I have done that with the best of them, over the years. I have done my fair share of rolling around on the floor and laughing hilariously and doing various things like that, which has been all part of my journey.

'Living loved' is a state of pure bliss but has many different expressions: sometimes it has the appearance of drunken stupor but not always. I feel loved and in bliss whatever my external appearance. If you need an external experience every time to actually encounter God and go to heaven, then you are going to struggle to make it a lifestyle. Bliss is a state of mind which is not always an externally noticeable or demonstrative experience. It is our state of reality that counts not just the external appearances: to be able to be a godlike being, living in the spirit as a normal part of our lives. God wants our living in the spirit to be very normal and natural-but-supernatural, and we can all learn how.

If we are taught about mystical experiences at all, it is usually that all these things happen in a trance-like state. Now, I have to be honest, in the beginning, a lot of it did happen to me in a trance, but the trance was not something I induced or even looked for. I would not recommend doing that at all. What I found subsequently was that I could engage in heaven without that, which is really helpful. You cannot afford to go into a trance or be so whacked in the Spirit when you are driving down the road that you lose control. If you do, either you or other people are going to be in serious trouble as a result of you crashing.

Zechariah 3:1-7 talks about a journey from walking in His ways to standing in His presence. That is the journey God wants us all to take. To learn to walk in His ways here, but eventually to stand in His presence, having gone through several other stages: having access to His courts, ruling His house and operating with authority in the Kingdom.

I have gone from having many encounters with His presence to standing in His glory. Those experiences are so different. I believe that when we see the glory of God manifest among us that will make things very much more objective, rather than subjective. I have been in meetings where I had amazing times with God and later heard other people talk about how boring it was. That is what I mean by 'subjective': it depends on what frame of mind you are in so that one person's wonderful meeting is another person's boring meeting. But when God turns up in person, when His glory cloud appears tangibly so that everyone can see it, there will be no doubt. God wants to move us from presence in our meetings to glory when we gather. That will change a lot of things. This is when heaven and earth are in such overlap that we will not know if we are in heaven or heaven is on earth. The days are coming when we are going to learn to live continually in the spiritual realms and be quantum entangled with our soul and body on the earth.

In the Old Testament, when the glory cloud filled the temple, the priests could not stand to minister, whereas Jude talks about standing in the glory (Jude v24). We will have to get used to being able to minister in the glory of God and to radiate that glory ourselves. That is going to take some time. When we first started experiencing heavy manifestations of God's glory in our meetings here, hardly anyone could stand up under it. Most people were flat on their faces. I don't know how our musicians managed to play at all. We called it TWOMP, The Weight Of My Presence.

Now we have learned to minister in that presence. We tend to forget what it was like when we were first getting used to standing in that environment when the glory of God begins to manifest, yet other people come in and they are on their faces before God as we were. We are going to see more of it.

My journey is from having visions, to having visitations, to living in that realm. I believe that is what God wants all of us to do because that is what Jesus did. The reason He was able to do all He did was that He lived in that heavenly spiritual realm and in this earthly realm at one and the same time.

This journey is from engaging the dead letter of the written word to engaging the living spiritual letters and living in an intimate relationship with Jesus the living Word. I used to read the Bible right through in a different version every year. I read it and read it and read it. I have a really good deposit of scripture within my spirit. But I hardly ever read it that way at all now. I just want to talk to the living Word. Why read about things in a book when you can go and talk to Him face to face? He does not need to speak to me through something He has written in a book.

When I was away at college, Deb and I wrote love letters to each other; I still have some of them. It would be very strange indeed if I opened them each morning and began speaking to her only using what had been written in a letter.

Please don't misunderstand me; I am not saying that I do not honour the Bible. I love the Bible and I use it a lot, especially in teaching, because it is a really good basis for getting to know God. In a way, it gives us a starting point, but it is only an introduction to a relationship, and it is the relationship God truly desires: relationship with Him, and not with a book. We have been so caught up in the written word, as a letter rather than as a person. Jesus is the living Word of God. I would rather go and talk to Him and ask Him things than just read about it.

Some people will be aghast at this and will see it as heresy to say that I do not have to read the Bible. But I carry the word of God in my heart all the time because He has written it there. Those things that I have learned to engage and have revelation of, they are now written on the tablets of my heart. They are not on a piece of paper.

My journey has been one from studying the Bible avidly as 'the word of God' to rarely reading it at all but having a living relationship with Jesus as the Word. I believe God wants us all to experience that living, active person, to be able to talk to Him, listen to Him and have Him in our lives as a reality.

I will expand on my journey with this in another thread.

So this journey for me has been one of letting go of the old, much of which was good, and embracing the new, which is the best. I would not give up what I am living in now for anything, other than for more of God and deeper relationship because there is always going to be more with God.

For those of you who would say that you do already know God, please understand that I would have said the same. But really we know only a fraction of who God is. He is revealing Himself more and more as we continue to grow in that relationship with Him.

My journey is from reading about God in the Bible to living with Him on a daily basis. I believe that is what God wants for all of us. It is a journey from seeing to living in the Spirit. I have learned to see in the Spirit, but I want to continue living in the Spirit.

In Revelation 1, John says he was in the Spirit. He was living in the realm of the Spirit. That is part of where my journey goes. My journey goes from visiting the house of God, which most of us do, to being a house of God, which all of us are. We already know it deep down but we have to have our minds deconstructed and renewed to be able to experience true reality.

It is a journey which starts from where my eyes had not seen (1 Corinthians 2:9), to where my eyes have seen a revelation in intimacy and personal experience. My eyes have seen; my ears have heard; my heart is the garden of delights. I have learned to engage God in my heart, in the garden of my heart.

In this journey, I have discovered so much about who I am, as well as who God is. Now I can have daily, face to face relationship with God who is in me because I am His house. He lives in me so I can engage Him in His house and He engages me in my house. Both experiences are equally as personal, intimate and real because my spirit is a real place. So is my soul, and both of them are dimensional places that are bigger than our body. If you are familiar with the BBC series *Doctor Who*, you will know that the Tardis in which he travels is bigger on the inside than the outside. Our spirit and soul are like that. So in the garden of your heart, you can have things which are way bigger than could fit in your own heart, (that is, in the living, beating organ in your chest). I have mountain ranges in the garden of my heart, lakes and forests, things that I have planted. We are supposed to look after it, tend it and cultivate it. I didn't even know I had it, as I shared more fully in the thread on fatherhood and sonship.

My journey has had many stepping stones and significant milestones. Many of the things that I share, like hearing God's voice, having visions, seeing in the Spirit, Spirit travel and heavenly encounters may all seem really easy when I share them. They are really normal for me now, but it has been a long journey of discovery to get here. God has shown me many things over many years that have been stepping stones to getting where I am now. I am certain that there will be many more significant encounters to come if I am to be a fully mature son of God.

I have been on this journey as a forerunner. As a forerunner, you have to press through, overcome, and then open the door for other people. That is what a forerunner does. You have experiences that will open the door for other people, who may then have greater experiences. I love talking to people who have done things that I have never done in heaven because I learn from them.

I do lots of online video hangouts with people all around the world. I love hearing things that cause me to think "Wow, I am going to go and find that place. I am going to go there because I have not been there." There have been a lot of things that I have learned to do that way. Desire is cultivated in our hearts, and that begins to open up the possibilities to encounter the reality if we are willing to pay the cost: usually surrendering self and spending the necessary time to incubate desire within intimacy.

First encounter

In 1993 we had an outpouring of the Spirit in the church. This was pre-Toronto, and therefore very, very controversial because no one had heard of anything like it. It started with a video someone had of a Rodney Howard-Browne meeting. They played it in one of our house meetings, and everyone collapsed into a heap of laughter and wildness.

This went through the church like wildfire and we had so many wild and wacky kinds of experiences. It did open up a number of visions, such as the mountain vision I mentioned before, but they were all involuntary, nothing I could do out of choice, they just happened.

I didn't have any grid of reference for most of it. Those days were just a lot of fun, of God wooing His church and calling the church back into intimacy. That was really the beginning of my journey into intimacy, it started with laughter and then went deeper and deeper from there.

In 2002, I had an encounter with God which now - when I look back - was one of the most significant things that have happened to me. It was nothing spectacular on the surface but was the origin for so much of what followed. It was really an encounter with the living Word versus the written word and my introduction to meditation. I had no desire to meditate and no understanding of meditation or anything like that whatsoever.

Then one day God spoke to me (and by that I mean that I had a feeling, an impression or thought that I knew was not mine) and asked, "Why do you use your Bible as a filing cabinet?" The thought came straight to my mind. My reaction was, "I don't". He said, "Open it". So I opened it and there were all the highlights and underlined passages and so on. And He said, "How much of that do you actually know by experience?"

I was gutted, because I had underlined all these things, highlighted all these things, but how many of them was I living by? How many of those verses were my personal experience? So I began a journey of learning how to meditate on Bible passages. I stopped reading the whole Bible through every year. Instead, God would highlight a verse, just one at a time, and I would focus on that one verse, sometimes for weeks or even months, until I had sucked every bit of truth and life out of it that I could.

The first one He drew to my attention was Joshua 1:8, and it was a key one because in it God talks about meditating and the results of meditation, which was really helpful:

This book of the law shall not depart from your mouth, but you shall meditate on it day and night, so that you may be careful to do according to all that is written in it; for then you will make your way prosperous, and then you will have success.

Another was 2 Corinthians 9:8, and I spent weeks in that verse:

And God is able to make all grace abound to you so that always having all sufficiency in everything; you may have an abundance for every good deed;

All I did was allow the Spirit of God to bring life and revelation from Him by just allowing it to go round and around my mind, repeating it, speaking it out, a word at a time. No one taught me to do it. I just took a step of obedience and did what I felt. It totally changed how I heard God speak to me and how He encountered me. It opened up the reality of what was written for it to become a living experience.

Meditating this way was having the Spirit speak to me in my mind about what I was reading and it was like the thoughts of God dancing in my mind. That's what it felt like. It opened up the truth and the revelation of the words on the page, making them come alive. All of a sudden the thoughts of God were not just filling my mind; I started to have a personal conversation with God within my mind. I began to talk to God, He began to talk to me, and we had conversations. These conversations were as real as any interactions I had with people in the natural realm.

That was a huge change from when I used to carefully study a chapter or two and get a good sermon out of it or maybe sometimes I would pray. I used to pray all the time, but it would be asking God for things. My prayer relationship, as for a lot of us in the past, only amounted to asking God, "Can You do this? Can You do that? I've got this need, someone else has a need, can You help them?"

In reality, there was very little of listening to what God was saying. He didn't get a chance to say much because I kept talking, usually with a shopping list of things I wanted Him to do. Now things were very different. My praying became a conversation where He spoke to me and I heard Him speaking; it was a radical change and a major milestone on my journey.

It opened up the possibility of a real relationship; because you cannot have a relationship with someone you do not talk to or listen to. Even in the absence of a real relationship God still gets through to us one way or another, because He really, really does want to speak to us and He really wants us to hear Him. So He will use a lot of other things like Bible verses, or nature, or other people to speak to us. All the while what He really wants is to have a conversation with us personally and intimately. Nowadays I can talk to Him and know that He is going to answer. His answers are often questions and are always what I need to hear rather than what I want to hear. What I like to do the most is hang out with Him and listen.

I would not ask Him things that are really 'out there' to start with because you have to learn to discern His voice among all the others that are competing for space in your head. By the way, all this does happen in your head, and that is not a problem. People will object and say "Everything you're talking about, it's all in your head" and I'll say, "Yes, it is". There's no big deal about that. Everything happens in our head, whether it is a vision, whether we are in heaven, having a first-person experience, whatever. We still see it or perceive it all in our head and encounter it all in our brain, in our imagination. That's where it works. That is where all the electrical impulses from our eyes, ears and all our senses, physical, emotional or spiritual are interpreted. That reality is one we really need to embrace.

So over time, I have learned to have this personal conversation with God. Now I do ask him a lot of really intricate things, and He tells me a lot of things I really don't understand. I made the mistake once of asking him to explain love. He spoke to me for about an hour. Afterwards, I still didn't understand anything He had said. It was in English, and I recognised the words, but it made no sense to me because He was talking to me in terms I just didn't have any grid for at the time. I wrote it all down - and I strongly recommend you do the same - and I have gone back over it, over the years. When I look at what I wrote down now, I understand much more of what He was saying and recently much of it has come into focus.

At Freedom we do a lot of work in the community with disadvantaged people, homeless people, and those with addictions, so in 2005 I went to a conference in London for churches interested in social enterprise. I went to learn more about how to help people get back into employment and how to use businesses to fund our vision. There was one session I was really looking forward to. The speaker got up and said, "I was going to talk about this (the advertised subject that I had come to hear about), but actually I really feel we need to do something else instead. We are going to learn how to meditate and see God."

I became really annoyed. I had travelled four hours up from Devon especially to listen to this particular seminar on something God was calling us to do in our community, and now the guy was going to do some stupid meditation, some kind of visualisation exercise. I had a really bad attitude.

And then God said, "I asked him to do that just for you". I felt undone and disarmed. I told Him I was really sorry.

The speaker was a Church of England vicar, and he just led a simple exercise about activating your imagination to see. The exercise was about walking on a beach and it was perfect for me, having grown up in a seaside town with five beaches. I discovered that I could do it, much to my surprise, because even though I had engaged in the thoughts of God and could talk to Him, it had never really occurred to me that I might actually be able to see Him. That might sound really stupid, but I would just talk to Him, He talked to me, and I listened. Now suddenly I began to see with my imagination. I still use that exercise to help people start to see with their imagination.

The eyes of my heart were activated and the lights were turned on. I had had pictures and visions previously that were involuntary gifts of the Holy Spirit but now I was able to see.

This set me on a journey in which I began to actually encounter what was in the Bible, which was where I started. I started to mediate visually on a passage and then enter into that reality. I entered in by experience, by picturing it, visualising it and seeing it. To start with it was snapshots and pictures, which was pretty cool at the time.

I can remember the very first time it became something that was so real that it shocked me. One day I was meditating on Jesus and His disciples, they were sitting down in a group and Jesus was talking to them. I thought "I'm going to picture that". I pictured it and I sort of sat there, in this scene and then Jesus looked at me, like really looked at me, as if he could see me. I thought "He can see me!" Then he spoke to me and asked me a question, in this scene. It was like 'wow'. This was really when the written word became alive, a living and active reality. Then I realised I could engage it, experience it and see it. It was real, and real to me; however God wanted me to go further and actually engage it.

I then found many really wonderful chapters which were visual and experiential. Psalm 23 was the one that really got hold of me. I think if you live Psalm 23, you do not need anything else in the Bible at all. You have everything you need in that psalm because it is all about our relationship with God as our shepherd.

I learned I could lie down in a green pasture beside quiet waters. I learned He was my shepherd and that He would restore my soul, which was an amazing place. To relax and lie down and allow God to restore your soul without having to do anything was just amazing. I just gave Him more and more opportunities by spending time resting in that place of intimacy in my soul. I found my good Shepherd started to restore my soul and make it whole. That was a really wonderful experience. I did not know where this was at the time but now I know I can engage God in the gardens of heaven or of my own heart.

Desires of your heart

God seems to hijack me at conferences. I went to another one in 2008, about working with the police in the community. We had a Chief Constable in one of our police force regions who was an active Christian. He was going, invited by a Christian ministry, Redeeming our Communities, so another local Christian police officer and I went along too. But again, the subject of the conference was nothing to do with anything that happened for me.

The first night, Debra Green, who was running the conference, asked if anyone would like prayer. I am always up for prayer so I went up near the front of the line. She laid hands on me but I didn't feel anything. Normally I am really sensitive to the Spirit but I didn't feel a thing. She started prophesying, "God has seen the desires of your heart." Then my ears pricked up. I had been preaching on John 14:12 for two years, had started to do some of the works of Jesus in a small way, but had not experienced the fullness of the reality of doing the works of Jesus and greater works.

When she said that God had seen the desires of my heart, I knew those desires were to see the works of Jesus and greater works. I thought "This prophecy is genuinely from God". And she then started to prophesy "God has put a healing anointing on you. He's going to break addictions and He's going to do miracles, and you will have an increase in the supernatural". I thought, "I will take all of that". I did not feel anything physically, nothing at all, but I took it by faith.

This was on a Thursday. I got home and the first thing I did at the Sunday meeting before we did anything else was give this away. I stood and shared the testimony of what I had received.

I said "I don't believe it is just for me, I believe it is for us. Would anyone else like this?" What happened next was totally unexpected. I thought a few people would come forward (probably the usual suspects) but everyone just ran up to the front. The power of God fell on the place, more than I had ever seen anywhere, and I have been around many moves of the Spirit. The power of God just absolutely fell. Initially it was characterised by many people having visions but subsequently we saw an increase in healing, an increase in the number of people coming to faith and getting free from addictions.

Portal

But it was the visions and prophetic revelations that struck me the most. So I decided to do some prophetic workshops and teach people how to prophesy and get words of knowledge. We had great fun exploring the prophetic realm and trying out the exercises you get in prophetic books. We had people stand behind one another and prophesy over them without knowing who they were. There was an older guy, Alan, who at the time said that he could not see anything. He did not give up and although he struggled with the prophetic exercises, later on when heaven opened up he learned to see with his activated imagination. Now he sees clearly in the spiritual realm; he sees angels and living creatures and often sees and talks with Jesus.

On one Monday evening, I stayed late after work. I was sitting at my desk thinking, "We have a prophetic workshop tonight" so I began to ask God to really come and help people see and hear. I think that was the first time I actually lost consciousness of what was going on around me. My desk opened up as a portal appeared and I got sucked into it. This was in September 2008. It would be what I now consider my second heavenly encounter. I could only assume that I went into heaven through the portal because at the time I did not really know. I had not been there like that before.

Eventually, I found I was beside the river of fire. It was amazing: I was there fully immersed in a first-person encounter. Everything was living and active, vibrant colours, intense fragrances, all my senses enhanced. I was shocked and it took me a while to focus. I knew enough to know there is a river of fire and it flows out of the throne of God. So where was the throne of God? I got the impression that the throne of God was up there somewhere but there was this big river of fire in front of me. I thought "How do I get up there? How do I bridge this river?" and I saw a construction in my mind that was intricate like a scaffold but just collapsed as soon as I attempted to climb it.

As soon as I stopped trying to work it out, nine steps just appeared, leading up to that throne. Now, I know what they are, the fire stones that are talked about in Ezekiel 28, in the garden of God, the mountain of God.

You were in Eden, the garden of God... You were the anointed cherub who covers, And I placed you there. You were on the holy mountain of God; you walked in the midst of the stones of fire (Ezekiel 28:13, 14).

Even now I cannot really describe it, as it was like nothing I had ever seen even in science fiction films. It was just like looking into a swirling mix of colour, like I was looking into the sub-atomic structure and seeing the particles swirling with waves of grace and faith. I was just looking intently at this amazing sight but I could not help thinking, "I want to get to that throne. I just have to get up those steps."

How did I know they were swirling with grace and faith? Sometimes you just know things in heaven. You just know that you know. I was looking at it and thinking, "Hey, that is grace and faith. I am going to take a step by grace and faith."

As I took that first step onto the first tread it felt like I became one with it. Literally I just merged with, became combined with and one with this fiery step which was love. I had never ever felt love like this – not even the time I felt as if liquid love got poured into me when I got baptised in the Spirit. This was like I was love. I became joined with the step. I don't know how long I stayed there from a heavenly perspective because it was just so amazingly wonderful. This was beyond emotion, but in my spirit I desired to see that throne. Eventually, I got myself to take another pace forward onto the next step and – wow! – it was joy. I then started to figure out that this might be the fruit of the Spirit. It was like I was joined with joy. This was not like laughter joy, this was just pure joy at the deepest level and I was joy. I had never experienced anything like this. It was the deepest sense of absolute joy; that is the only way I can describe it.

So I stayed there in another moment of "Wow! This is amazing", but still I wanted to get up to that throne. Eventually, I took each step and they became peace, patience and all the fruit of the Spirit as an experience, and a fragrance, a colour, and everything of heaven just became real. Every step was more than an experience; it was more a 'being', in the sense that I *was* love, joy and peace and my whole being encapsulated it.

Eventually, I got up to the top of the steps. There was the throne of God, and I could not even look at it. All I could see were the feet of God. I just could not look up. So there I was, on my face, looking at His feet, absolutely in awe. I couldn't look at His face or anything else. I felt transfixed; not exactly fearful but certainly awestruck. As I kept looking I saw Jesus' feet next to the Father's. I know the scripture says that Jesus sits at the right hand of the Father, so it made sense in a bizarre kind of way.

I was having a jumble of thoughts, unable to make sense of this sensory overload. Then one thought broke through: "I wonder, do I have a throne somewhere?" I looked off to the side and I could see multitudes of thrones all going off into the distance. I started to crawl away, not looking up until I could get up. When I did, I saw all these amazing thrones. So I started walking along, and as far as I could see, there were thrones. Sadly most of them had no people sitting on them but were occupied by what I assumed were their angels, though there were two people I recognised.

So I kept walking until I eventually found my throne. This is the throne where I am seated in heavenly places. My throne was not elaborately decorated, more functional, but my name was inscribed there - not 'Mike' but my sonship identity as a heavenly name. I am not going to tell you what it is because it is very personal to me. Once I found it I sat down and immediately I was right next to Jesus, just immediately connected to Him and He was right next to the Father.

I was on His right hand and He just reached down and grabbed my hand. Now He had my hand in His. So there I was, seated on my throne, and then I had another overwhelming experience: a huge oval screen opened up right in front of me, and on it the most amazing vision in 3-D, high definition, or I could say 4K or 8K, ultra-high definition picture. The colours were just intense. I was looking at things that were familiar to me: I could see where I lived, I could see our whole area, but it was all absolutely sharp and multi-coloured from a heavenly perspective. It was absolutely amazing. I was looking at it and then the whole screen turned around and I could see the same scene in dull grey tones.

I just felt, "That's how I see it all the time, because I am always looking at it from earth". When you look at it from heaven, it looks so different. You are seeing it from a perspective of how God's purposes are intended for it. This was like really, really real. I was there. It was not like a vision. I was just there, doing all these things, and engaging all these things.

Then I saw a portal open up and an angel standing beside it. The portal was like a whirlpool of golden liquid. I saw the glory of God just pouring out, down through this portal and the angel was just standing there. I was thinking, "Are you going to show me something?" So I was looking at it and he took me down through the portal into the atmosphere around the earth. I could look up and down and saw a golden glory waterfall. I then saw three demonic, hideous-looking things, not very big creatures, and they just blocked it off. They were able to turn off the flow like shutting off a tap so it seemed just to backup beyond what I could see. I was gutted. An overwhelming sadness came over me.

Then the angel said, "This is what happens every time a portal gets opened; it can be blocked off". I asked why and he said "Because you block it off". He was not talking about me personally but about us, about people. When the glory of God gets poured out and we get what we call revival, a move of

God, we always mess it up one way or another. Through falling out with one another, through relational issues, through jealousy, competition; whatever happens to authorise those beings to block it off. I was really, really annoyed at that.

Immediately I came back to my desk. In earthly time it took about an hour or so. But in heavenly time (because there is time in heaven, it is just different) it was a lot longer. It seemed to be a long time, in fact each one of those steps felt like hours – and there were nine of them.

Forty day fast

Now that I had had that experience I started to think, how do I get more? I wanted that again and I did not know how. I was so frustrated that I couldn't get back to it. I thought maybe it was just one of those sovereign things that God did. But I did everything I could. I got Patricia King's *Glory School* book and tried everything. I searched the internet for anything that said how to get into heaven and I tried every one of them. None of it worked but I continued to pursue it. I did not let it go. And as I continued to pursue it I became increasingly hungry for it.

So it was at this point, in May 2010, that my friend Mike Bryant, who is a very prophetic guy and quite an interesting character, sent me the letter I mentioned in the previous thread. I read it and it said, "I have seen your heart". I immediately wondered "Wow, what's coming? For two years I have been waiting to get back into heaven, and God knows my heart."

It went on: "A change is coming and you can't stop it. So be strong in my Spirit and the things I have shown you. Prepare for the future and know that the harvest you long for is near.

Ascend to where I am, where you are seated, and a door will open for you. Prepare for the future, ask of me and I will show you".

Now there was one phrase in there that really got my attention. I knew what "where you are seated" meant and I thought "This is going to be really good". So I got extremely excited by this. On the envelope Mike had written that I should read it once a day for 49 days, so I thought "Okay, I can do that".

Soon after, in June 2010, came the conference with Stacy Campbell and Ryan Wyatt. This was the time God spoke to me really clearly on the way and said, "This conference is for you and me. I don't want you to talk to anybody or pray for anyone or be ministered to by anyone. I just want you to come and meet with me."

It was not too far, about 75 miles away, so I thought I would just drive down for the day and come back. I ended up staying for three. It totally changed my heart and transformed my heart's desire. As soon as the worship began I was captivated with God's heart. It wasn't anything that anyone said, though they said some good things. Stacey Campbell shook a lot and Ryan Wyatt was great, but actually, I just met God in the worship in a level of intimacy that I had never felt before.

Over those three days I became more desperate for God than I had ever been. I came home and everything felt different. On the way home in the car, God said, "I want you to do a forty day fast." My reaction was that was no problem. I didn't even think about it being forty days, though I think the longest fast that I had previously done was seven days.

I shared with the leadership that I really felt God wanted me to do a forty day fast, but He wanted me actually to be on my own for the forty days. They said, "Okay, great, do it, we will fast along with you by getting someone to fast each day".

So on August 1st 2010 I took to my room with a water cooler and lots of books, soaking music and my laptop to record the fast on a blog to share with the church.

God spoke to me and said to pray in tongues for the first hour of each day and I read the prophecy Mike Bryant had sent me and meditated on it every day. I had so much revelation as I read the Bible. The whole Joshua Generation teaching came from this time, along with so much truth about grace and many other subjects. I wrote those things as I blogged my experiences day after day.

But I was still not getting into heaven. I was seeking God and playing soaking music, doing everything I could possibly think of. Ryan Wyatt produced some videos of engaging God with a music accompaniment. I played them and it did not do a thing. I was thinking, "What am I doing wrong? It must be something".

The strangest thing was that I was literally burning. I thought, "Great. I was expecting to get back into heaven, but I have ended up just being burnt!" Physically, other than my face, everything was just red hot, like literally burning. It felt like my very bones were burning.

I was experiencing that depth of fire every night, so I didn't really sleep for twenty-one nights and I was not eating. Yet I received so much revelation from reading the Bible. I wrote reams and reams of things that now are really useful. I found that it gave a foundation for many of the things that I was going to experience.

I asked God to show me anything that was going to be a hindrance. I renounced everything He showed me, in fact everything I could possibly think of. That is how I spent most afternoons during that first period of the fast.

Then on day nineteen I was lying down on a sofa in the window of my room when I fell into a trance. I literally went into a complete trance. It felt like I was sinking into the sofa. I went into heaven, finally had a first person experience in heaven again. And over the next three weeks, I was to journal eighty-seven different heavenly encounters and visions.

That first encounter was bizarre and lasted for hours in earthly time but perhaps days in heavenly time. I experienced so many encounters and places that it took me five hours to write down the gist of my experience. My hand was cramped at the end of it, but it was worth it because I really didn't want to forget any of it.

The first thing that I had was a quantum physics lesson. Although I was a scientist, I really hated physics because it was theoretical. Chemistry was great, because you could make explosions, and biology was great, too, because you got to cut things up and dissect things. So I was into all that, but physics I just found boring.

I was going to do physics at A-level stage, but I chickened out and did geology instead. Well, now I had a quantum physics lesson from God, the creator and sustainer of all things, and it was far from being boring! He showed me how the spiritual and physical dimensions interact and how they are connected, what the quantum realm is, and how that is connected. This was just weird for me because it was something I knew nothing about at all.

Zero point energy, creative light, created light: I was actually seeing into the micro-realm of how things work. It is very difficult to describe unless you have seen it. It was literally around me, energy, particles and waves; how things get made and how matter and energy get transformed. I was just in it beyond anything that I could have imagined or thought. I engaged the speed of light, but on a timeline, and went back in time.

God taught me about string theory. String theory is also referred to as 'the theory of everything', it is about how everything holds together. He told me "My grace is the vibrating power that's in everything, as the voice of creation". Until that point I didn't know anything about string theory. It was a term I had heard but knew nothing about, and later on I researched what scientists were saying about it and what it meant. What it meant was exactly what He told me, only He put it in terms of His grace, being His divine power in everything, vibrating and holding the whole creation together. So you can find string theory in Ephesians 4:6. He is in and over and through all things and He is keeping everything together by the voice of His power, which is still vibrating at the frequency that He spoke when he created it all.

He took me into different dimensions, heavens, earth, under the earth. At that point in time, I was pretty clueless about where any of what I experienced took place. It was just overwhelming experience that I encountered. Fortunately, I remembered enough of it to write it down later, because I certainly couldn't write it down while I was having the experience because I was totally immersed in it. I wasn't aware of my natural surroundings at all. As far as I could tell, I was really there.

Jesus talked to me about frequency, resonance and harmony. I knew enough to know that those are musical terms. He said, "You need to understand how frequency, resonance and harmony work because once you understand how they work, you will be able to do things you cannot now do". He went into it in quite a lot of depth.

He took me back and showed me creation being spoken into existence. That was just the most amazing thing, to see how it was spoken out. He took me out into another solar system. These experiences were just really weird. Why did I need to see another solar system?

Most of the time you can go to a heavenly place in an instant, but this was a journey that was taking time and covering distance: I was moving quite fast but going out into the solar system, then into the stars and into another solar system. I saw a planet with vertical rings and it was amazing, but what was the point?

He asked me if I had noticed anything on the way. Was I supposed to? I had noticed lots of things, and they were awe-inspiring, but it was only when He drew my attention to it that I realised we had been flying through space and there was no darkness. That is what He wanted me to recognise: there was no darkness, so this was what it was like before it got messed up.

Then He took me back and showed me what the first creation was like on earth before Satan came and spoiled it. I saw where there was no absence of light which was amazing. He then revealed various things about frequency, what was lost at the fall, the flood, Babel: all the supernatural abilities we had that were lost but will be restored.

At the end of this encounter God spoke to me and said "Now I want you to go and hear Ian Clayton". Who was Ian Clayton? I looked him up on the internet and found out that he was actually speaking that same night in Torquay, seventy-five miles away, in the same venue that I had been to for the Ryan Wyatt conference.

I did not think I could drive seventy-five miles safely after nineteen days of fasting. So I emailed everyone in the church, saying "This is a guy who trans-relocates around the world and he is speaking tonight in Torquay" to see if I could get a lift. I had found a YouTube video of him teaching about trans-relocation and I thought that was really cool.

Someone said they would take me and in fact about a dozen of us went down to hear him. Ian was there for two nights and rather than teaching he was in machine gun mode. If you have ever heard him speak, you will know exactly what I mean. He just sprayed out all this revelation and all of it was about things that I had just experienced that day. It was all about the spiritual realm and I thought "Wow, okay, I have not lost my mind". It was all very helpful in confirming that I really wasn't mad, because it had been such a weird encounter.

Ever since I had that initial breakthrough, with the exception of a four month period in the dark cloud in 2011/12 which is part of another thread, I have experienced first person encounters every single day. Every day I have engaged in the supernatural spiritual realms of heaven and within my own spirit and soul. That was 7 years ago. At first I visited heaven every day and those encounters in heaven were visitations, but now I have learned to live there permanently.

I began to sense the amazing harmony of heaven: it is just overflowing, abundant in every way at a deeply intense level. Everything has enhanced colours, frequency and sound, fragrance and emotions. When you step on the grass, you feel it, sense the fragrance of it, the emotion and peace. Everything is harmoniously flowing together in unity and oneness as if it just knows its place and is totally content and at rest.

We are familiar with our five senses but there our senses are all heightened, there are more of them and everything is in oneness. Everything is living, everything is vibrant. Everything is living in a state of perfection, living as it was always intended, and you can feel it. I have grown more used to it now but it is still awesome and sometimes wondrous to just walk in the heavenly realms.

I have seen so many things that are difficult to describe, but I found images online by a young girl called Akiane Kramarik, who has seen heaven and painted much that is similar to what I had seen: the quantum reality, what you see at a sub-atomic level of being, how it is all held together and how creation is spoken out into existence, how all the mountains go out first because they are the symbols of authority and the place of government.

There were several pictures she had painted at which I just thought, "Yes, this is what I have seen". Again, that was really affirming. The picture she painted of Jesus, the Prince of Peace, was exactly how I saw Him. As soon as I saw that painting I thought, "That's Him! That's Jesus!" Other people might see Him differently but that's exactly how I saw Him. There was a movie I watched called "Heaven is Real". In it there was a little boy who had been to heaven and when he saw Akiane's painting of Jesus he said the same thing, "That's Him!" It really is. She has such an amazing gift, not only to be able to engage in heaven but also to paint what she sees. I have trouble even describing it, let alone painting it, and she can put those amazing landscapes and images onto canvas. Her work is truly remarkable, especially when you consider that she was only around six to ten years of age when she was producing it and having all those remarkable encounters.

Like Paul, who said that some of these things are inexpressible, I sometimes just get lost for words. Some of the things Paul saw, he could not express because he did not have access to the modern parables and analogies of science and quantum physics. There simply are no words to describe an experience when you don't have a grid of reference for it here. Even though you go there and experience it, and know what you are experiencing, the words to describe it just don't exist.

When someone else has experienced something, and we talk about it together, then although we might describe it differently we resonate and have this inner knowing that yes, we are talking about the same thing. But when I first came out and started sharing with others, they were perplexed because they had never experienced anything remotely like it. Once I started to open up that realm and other people went through the door and began finding the reality of some of this for themselves, then suddenly they could grasp what I had been saying because they now had their own experience of it.

Someone else's words or testimony can be an encouragement to pursue something, but you cannot just base everything on that, you have to experience it yourself.

Jesus engaged me in so many different ways during the fast and even more since.

Some of them were very symbolic. In one encounter Jesus was just kneeling in front of me and I walked up to Him. His arms were out as if He wanted to give me a hug. I was walking very stiffly, and when I looked down I was wearing a suit of armour. He looked at me and said, "You can't hug Me like that. You don't need that here". I have been hurt a lot in my life. I have been healed of so much but I was still guarded, and that armour was all my protection mechanisms. When He said, "You need to trust me," I surrendered and let it all just fall off.

Immediately I felt like a child with a renewed sense of innocence in His presence. And I noticed that I really did appear to be a little kid, standing in front of Him. Jesus took me by the hand and He lead me up some steps, like spiral stones going up to a castle. So we walked together and began ascending. As we got to the top, there was a large angel standing at a high bench with a book.

I just knew that this was the Book of Life and that my name had to be in it. As I stood there the angel was thumbing through it. It seemed like ages and I was somewhat alarmed, wondering why he could not find my name. I really hoped my name was in that book. Because I was just a little kid, I had the emotions of a child, looking up at this angel thinking how I really wanted to go in. I looked up and there was Jesus with a really big grin on his face, just having a joke at my expense.

Eventually, he let me in. I walked in and immediately I was an adult. I was in the realm of heaven and I had some amazing face to face encounters with Jesus and the Holy Spirit. Again, these encounters were not just visions, they were real. Whenever we were just hanging out together Jesus would ask me, "What do you want to know?" What a question! Each time, I just asked whatever popped into my mind, often along the lines of "How did You do such and such a miracle?" I know, there are all kinds of things I could have asked, and I thought of lots of them later, but I just kept asking Him things that came to me in that moment. He always told me or sometimes took me back in time and showed me. He showed me how He did many miracles by controlling the quantum realm with His thoughts. He "popped a qwiff"; that is, He collapsed the possibility into reality with His mind. He also controlled the vibrational energy of matter to transform it.

I asked Him how He walked on water. He said He could have done it by hovering over it but He didn't. "I was able to control the vibration of the water and it became solid when I put my feet on it". That gave me the understanding that we can learn how to control the vibration, the frequency of matter, because everything is just energy vibrating at a particular frequency. He showed me lots of miracles and how He did them.

We can all learn to operate in this realm using our authority as sons of God to control the frequency of matter. As a result, I know how to do a lot of things. That doesn't mean that I have done them, because I have had no reason to do them. I know how to disappear. I know how to walk through things and put my hand through things. Some people say "Why don't you do it then?" These things are not party tricks to validate ourselves or show off but only when we see what the Father is doing can we do the same. We can all learn how to operate like Jesus did. Jesus didn't do things by magic. I think a lot of Christians just think it is magic. People did not just get healed. How did Jesus heal them? Jesus saw what the Father was doing but it was not that He got a list of instructions. As a son, Jesus had the creative power to choose which way to fulfil the desires of the Father's heart. That is why Jesus healed in so many different ways. He spoke into their DNA to change and realign. He touched people, directing grace and faith to impart a charge of anointing to heal. We can all learn how to see what the Father is doing and creatively release God's heart.

One of my favourite times was when He sat down and taught me the truth. On one occasion He taught me from Matthew 11:28-30, about the seat of rest and government. The profound truth concerning rest and identity contained within those few inspirational verses became transformational and an integral part of my life. "All of you who are weary and heavy laden, come to me and find rest". I find there are weary and heavy laden people all over the world, who are doing things in their own strength, a form of DIY religion through which they are trying to please or appease God. Many people are still trying to affirm their identity from their works, all because they have not found the place of rest, where they can do things in the joy of God's strength.

It is rest for our souls. Our souls will never be at rest while they are in control. I had a long journey of getting my soul to surrender control. I went through a number of experiences that highlighted my need to let go.

I met Jesus in many different guises, as He does not always appear to us in the same way. My most intense experience was when I was taken on the timeline to meet Him when He was on the cross. One day I was with Jesus and then instantly I was transported and I was standing in front of the cross. As I was standing there in shock and awe Jesus lifted His head and looked right into my eyes. The intensity of those eyes, deep pools of love penetrating into the depths of my soul, began the journey of discovering the true nature of God as Love.

The depth of love in his eyes when He was looking at me standing in front of Him still has a really emotional effect on me when I think about it, because He stepped into the depth of my soul, into my darkness, into my brokenness. He took my place. When He cried out "My God, My God, why have you forsaken me?" He fully associated with the anguish of my soul's separation, shouting out my soul's cry, and did that for me. When you stand in front of the cross and you see what He is doing for you and you realise you are actually being represented there, and you are also dying there with Him, it has an amazing effect. The cross took on a whole different reality for me when I stood before it. Honestly, I know I was literally there.

I engaged with the Holy Spirit many times. Most people have an image of the Spirit as a dove, lovely and gentle. I have to tell you that to me the Holy Spirit is the most mischievous, fun and life-giving person, who took me flying in the heavenly realms to places just for the joy of it. The Holy Spirit exudes creativity; everything is about vibrant, abundant and overflowing life, filled with energy and so exhilarating.

Betrayal wounds

As I shared previously, engaging the Father was life-changing, removing the scar tissue of my father wound. That was just fantastic but the next day Jesus met me and asked "Are you willing to deal with your betrayal wounds?" I was just about to say "I have dealt with those" when I thought better of it. So I said, "Yeah, okay."

There were fourteen specific wounds of betrayal that happened in my life. They all came back to my mind and my emotions with intensity. I experienced each one of those memories and He healed and restored my heart. He revealed the root issue of judgment which occurred when I was twelve years old and I had just gone to a secondary school which was in another town. I had lost all but two of my friends, so they were important to me. We were hanging out together and found some plans in a comic book to build a cart or trolley so we agreed to get together the next weekend to build it. I was excited to do this together and had brought some of my father's tools. When we went to the shed they unveiled this brand new blue and red cart that they had built without me. I was gutted. I covered up my disappointment but I judged them and hardened my heart as I did not yet understand forgiveness. That judgment came upon me and it was like my life had a banner over it in the spirit realm, saying "Betray me". It was always those closest to me, including some very close friends and fellow church leaders. I renounced that judgment and when He healed those wounds it restored my heart and removed my barriers and walls of protection. That totally changed my ability to engage with people.

I have always chosen to be open with people about my life but there was a guardedness that meant I always felt alone even in a group of people because there was a deep-seated fear that they were going to betray me. This encounter was really intense but transformed my ability to engage and relate to people which is now a central part of my life. You can get some serious things done when you embrace these encounters. The more proactive you are, the easier it is. To begin with God had to come and raise issues with me, but now I go to Him and say "If there is anything you want to deal with, feel free".

In another encounter, as I was exploring the Garden of Eden, I met one of the cloud of witnesses. I had a real encounter with him: he had a spade and he was digging a hole. I asked him who he was and what he was doing. He said he was Jacob and he was digging a well. I was confused as I remembered that Abraham and Isaac had dug wells but I didn't know that Jacob had! I later discovered that Jacob's well was where Jesus met the Samaritan woman and talked about drinking living water (see John 4:13-14).

Jacob told me to go and read about his life, particularly about his experience in Genesis 28 where he saw the ladder going up into the open heaven with angels ascending and descending on it. He named the place Bethel, and described it as "none other than the house of God and the gateway to heaven".

Revelation came to me that really changed everything about how God was dwelling within me and that I could access heaven from within my spirit. It was a revelation of John 14, which is my favourite chapter in the Bible, about being in I am and I am being in me. The Father, Jesus and Holy Spirit come to us and make their home in us. We become a house of God and a gateway to heaven. We have that intimacy in relationship.

Jesus' words in Revelation 3:20, "Behold I stand at the door and knock", became a real experience. I could open that door on a daily basis. At this point, I didn't really understand anything about my First Love Gate and other gateways because I hadn't heard that teaching from Ian Clayton. God has given him a scroll with a diagram of the gateways of spirit, soul and body something like this:

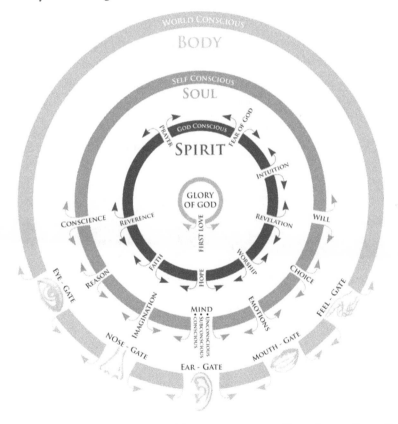

Fortunately, I had no problem opening my First Love Gate. I know some people struggle. They find it blocked or locked. For anyone who struggles to open that gate, it's just a projection of your soul, because it's your spirit. The enemy has no part to play in your spirit other than what he can deceive you into thinking, by projecting visions onto it.

I discovered the activation of my spirit and walked with Jesus through each of my spirit gates understanding what each gate is and how it functions.

A gateway is a place of authority where dominion is exercised so whoever controls our life's different gateways exercises authority, dominion and control over us. Our gates are designed to be open and flowing from the inside out so that we can become a gateway of heaven. Our eyes and ears and other physical senses are windows or gates to our soul. Our problems arise from the fact that up to now everything has always flowed from the outside in and we are conformed to that pattern – the world's mould. For us to be conformed to the heavenly pattern everything must flow from the inside out.

We may have inadvertently given demonic forces legal access and legal rights to sit in those gates so that they can now control, resist and block the flow. Or our ancestors may have done so and those rights may still be there. In either case we need to remove those legal rights and to cleanse, purify and rule our gates.

Familiar spirits can counterfeit gate functions for illegitimate purposes and often sit outside our spirit gates seeking to block the flow of the river of life flowing through us.

I learned to open my gates so that everything flows from the inside. I learned to be transformed from the inside out. Everything began to open up. I practised 45 minutes a day for a whole year to activate all those gateways, to understand them and have them all open and operating.

I systematically went through every year of my life for every gate in three weeks and I was wrecked. Every time I did four or five years at a time, I found patterns of sin and behaviour that were revealed as I went through the years of my life. Fortunately, I had just had all those love encounters, so there was no guilt or condemnation and I had no problem with owning it. I needed to deal with my soul gateways to discover the behavioural state of my conscience, mind, emotions, imagination and will, and why I make the choices I do.

As I went through each year of my life for each gate, I confessed and renounced the many things that were brought to my mind and I applied the blood of Jesus to each gate. The process totally changed my whole life. Everything began to flow from the inside out, from my spirit through my soul and out through my body. I began to interpret the things that I heard and saw through my natural senses from the perspective of my spirit, whereas before that mostly everything flowed from the outside in (and most of what went in that direction messed me up).

This revelation totally changed my perspective on where life came from within me. Opening that First Love Gate when Jesus knocks and inviting His presence into my spirit is something I still do every day. I began to take more notice of the construct of my spirit and could see that my spirit is like a mountain, with the river of life flowing from my First Love Gate and cascading down to spirit gates. The First Love Gate is access to the kingdom of God within us and was in what looked like a shimmering pillar, a portal or wormhole. This gate gives God access into our spirit and gives us access to the heavenly Garden of Eden.

I began to embrace the presence of God in my spirit. I have learned to connect with God as Father, Son and Spirit within my spirit in the intimacy of the relationship. I have learned to see how everything flows together. Now my gateways are just open and totally integrated. My spirit and soul work together. I went through many different processes to get my soul and ego to that point where it surrendered and I will go into more detail about that in the thread about the separation and reintegration of my soul and spirit

As my spirit grew in strength my soul's influence began to diminish and my spirit began to take a more prominent role in directing and guiding my life. Praying in tongues took on a new dimension as I learned to consciously pray out loud as well as in my mind but really accelerate things once I learned to continually pray as a bubbling effervescent fountain of life in my spirit. I would often find myself just flowing in tongues and rather than thinking "I am going to pray in tongues" by cognitive choice my spirit would just flow. Nowadays I often find myself just spontaneously doing things as my spirit leads. As I engaged first love I would drink living water, take the yoke of Jesus, abdicate from the seat of rest and invite the Father to father me. This is the reality of becoming joined to the Lord and one spirit with Him (1 Corinthians 6:17).

When you become joined to the Lord you can't tell whose spirit is your spirit or His spirit. You don't really know which you are being led by because it's just the spirit being one. It totally changes everything. Then you just do things as you are led and how your spirit leads rather than what you decide.

I found a lot of that works really well in heaven because you don't have to try and figure it out, you just let your spirit instinctively lead and direct.

There is a difference between the construct of my spirit where the kingdom resides and the consciousness of my spirit which can access any dimension in time and space and beyond.

After the 40 day fast I continued to have daily encounters with God both in my spirit and in the heavenly realms. These became intentional encounters rather than the involuntary experiences I had through being a trance or ecstatic encounter. I would choose to step into that spiritual realm by faith every day and those encounters were cognitive where soul and spirit would be actively involved. These were visitations where I would step in and step out because my soul needed to be cognitively involved. When my soul and spirit were separated and reintegrated then my spirit was able to continuously remain and inhabit those heavenly realms.

My journey took me from visions of heaven to visitations in heaven to a continual place of living in heaven and then I was able to live in a continual flow from heaven to earth. I can shift the focus of my soul's consciousness whenever I choose to focus on the natural or spiritual realm. This means I can describe things I am focused on although I am not seeing it as a vision in my mind. I know by a perceiving, by a stream of spiritual information, that my mind has learnt to interpret so that I can describe it visually or journal it.

Everything we relate to visually is received by our senses and interpreted within our brain on the screen of our imagination or by perception in thoughts. We develop the ability to decode electrical impulses or signals from all our senses, both physical and spiritual. Our physical senses receive electrical signals from our eyes and ears via our nervous system. Our spirit and our soul are both connected to the same system. We have the eyes and ears of our heart as well as our spirit. Our spirit and soul can project those images that are received and interpreted as images and thoughts within our mind. It is our imagination that is the screen that displays those visual images and perceptions. Our spirit resides in the cavity surrounding our brain and spinal cord and is separated from our blood system.

I learned to perceive as an information stream from my spirit. During my first encounters, I would journal them afterwards which often took quite a time. I then learned to journal while I was in encounters with my eyes open by interpreting the flow of spiritual information along that stream.

During my initial encounters in the heavenly and spiritual realms, I was engaging with Jesus and the Father in a place that I thought was heaven. It was a little place with a little bench, a small patch of grass, and a tree with a swing. I thought this was really great because I would sit on the swing and God would push me and we would talk or mostly I would listen. Sometimes we would sit on the bench and talk. I thought this must be a special place in heaven created just for me to hang out with God.

Then one day God said, "Do you know where we are?" I answered "Somewhere in heaven". He told me "We are in your heart, in your garden". I did not know you could meet with God there or that I even had a garden. Then I thought, "If this is my garden, is this all there is?" The more time I spent with God there, sometimes walking with Him and exploring like Adam did, the more the dimensions of my garden expanded.

I discovered a meadow area with a river running through it. That became a favourite place like the green pasture in Psalm 23 where I could sit and talk with the shepherd of my soul. It is a place where I love going because I can just rest, in the garden of my own heart, and look after it.

I have learned how to cultivate the garden of my heart now by using my creative consciousness to think things into being. I have the creative ability of God because I am made in His image. Once I discovered I could be creative in my garden, I had real fun forming things out of the desires of my heart. I can also plant seeds of my testimonies there in the good soil of my heart and water them from the river and command it to grow. I found that immediately trees grew and were laden with fruit. I discovered I could take the fruit and eat it to experience the testimony as a doorway to reengagement.

So now I have many new areas planted with colourful plants and many fruit trees, so my garden reflects my identity and my encounters. You may wonder how you know what you desire. You just have to let your imagination loose, start meditating and thinking and creativity begins to flow.

As I plant in the garden of my heart my heart reflects heaven and my experiences, so that they become testimonies. I can give that fruit away to others, and I do. That's why I do what I do in encounters and activations with people: I am actually giving them a taste of the fruit to inspire them to have their own encounters.

More and more people are now beginning to engage God in their own gardens. They are finding the river of life and all the wonderful things that are there. Hopefully they will get their own testimony of what they plant and can give their fruit away to others. That is what discipleship is, giving away what you have received. "Freely you have received, freely give" (Matthew 10:8). We must not be so precious with the experiences that we have had that we are not willing to give them away. There is nothing in heaven that I have ever encountered that I have not been willing to share, though sometimes I have not been able to share it until I have experienced it a number of times so that I could express it.

I want to give it away so that God will bless me with more. Many people keep things secret because knowledge is power. If people don't tell you things then they have more power than you. A lot of people don't give things away because of that. We need to be prepared to give everything away that God has given us because that's what we are supposed to do with it, bless others with it.

I have discovered so much that happens on the inside of us. We can have everything in the garden of our heart, we have encounters in heaven. We can have that as an ongoing personal testimony and experience that we can go back to, over and over again, that place of restoration.

As we learn to frame and shape the garden of our heart we are practising to learn to shape the world around by the power of our consciousness. If our gardens are patterned after heaven, then we have practice ground for when it comes to actually terraforming the planet. We need to restore it to original condition, which means we need to know how to speak, move, shift things, call things that are not as if they were (Romans 4:17) and be creative.

I have engaged with the river of life flowing in my heart but then flowing through me. I have learned to direct that flow of the river of life so that it doesn't stagnate but it flows out, to create the atmosphere of the Kingdom around my life. It can have different effects depending on which of the gates I direct it to flow through. The more our soul and spirit work together in unison the more instinctive and natural this lifestyle becomes.

I have discovered everything goes deeper. First love is deeper and deeper. After a while of practising this every day for years and years, I lost a little bit of the wonder of it and it became functional. I would open my First Love Gate and then think "What am I supposed to do today? What's my mandate? What am I authorized to do? Let's go to a mountain and rule". All that is good, but you need the relationship first.

When I started teaching this I was not planning to do a whole teaching module on the First Love Gate but just one session. God had other plans and for about three or four months, every time I opened my First Love Gate God hugged me and wouldn't let me go, every day. Every day I went deeper and deeper into the Holy Spirit; deeper and deeper into Jesus; deeper and deeper into the Father. Just deeper, and it was like being baptised into them, being clothed with them and knowing them out of a whole different level of personal relationship.

This was just a depth of personal communion and fellowship with the presence of God, Father, Son, Holy Spirit, and God himself in the sense of all three. You see, sometimes when you engage it's just God, but sometimes it's a very individual personality and you just know what you are experiencing is the Holy Spirit's embrace, or it is Jesus, and you just know that you know. They are different and you sense because they speak differently to you, they communicate differently and they share things differently.

After spending several years of daily engaging the heavenly realms I realised the more I knew, the more there was to know. When God started to hug me in first love I realised that I really knew nothing in light of God's infiniteness. I don't want to know anything apart from God because that knowledge will come from the wrong source, the DIY tree path. Even if the knowledge is good, it is still from the wrong source and has a negative effect.

My focus was on developing the relationship that would be foundational and fundamental to all responsibility and government.

During this time I began to explore the heavenly Garden of Eden to discover the amazing wonderful realm of such beauty filled with wonder and awe. It is a place where the atmosphere is filled with glorious love, joy and peace.

I discovered that after I opened my First Love Gate I could engage in heaven through that gateway within my own spirit. As we invite God's presence to dwell with us in the garden of our heart, He invites us into His heavenly garden by following the river of life back up through our First Love Gate. As the rivers of living water flow out of heaven and flow through our First Love Gate, we can follow it both into the garden of our heart and into Eden, heaven's garden. We can go back into those realms and find the source of everything we need in life. Just as God walked in the cool of the day with Adam, we can also walk with God in that place.

I discovered a heavenly pathway of relationship that I could walk on. I discovered I was a house of God, I was a place of intimacy and rest. I discovered I was a mountain and I had authority. I discovered I was a gateway of heaven and that it was supposed to flow through me to the world, just like the river that flowed out of Eden, into Adam's garden, and then flowed out as four rivers to water the earth.

I have rivers of living water that can flow through me if all those gateways of my spirit, soul and body are open. If they are not, it stagnates and doesn't go anywhere. It is like the Dead Sea. Nothing lives in the Dead Sea. A river has to flow out as well as in. There is no point in having the river flowing into our spirit if it can't flow out.

Most of us have lived with a trickle. God wants it to be a raging torrent turning into rivers of living water, bringing life wherever it goes. Ezekiel 47 is a picture of that. It can turn salt water into fresh. It can bring spiritual life if we allow it to flow from our innermost being. That flow from heaven's source can create an atmosphere of the Kingdom around us. We have to learn how to expand our boundaries, figuratively from Jerusalem to Judea, Samaria and the ends of the earth.

So I learned how to open my First Love Gate and engage in the realm of Eden and to experience God there. It's a wonderful, ongoing experience. When I first engaged the river of life in Eden I found that it went beyond earthly reality. It was crystal clear, not water as we know it (H_2O) but the essence of life itself, a distillation of the Spirit's essence and life source. You can breathe as you swim and float; the river flows through you and you can flow along with it. It is the most energising life-giving, enthralling experience and it doesn't stop there. There are many things floating in the river and at the bottom, such as gems, scrolls and items made of gold. Just as Ezekiel describes eating scrolls, we can eat these objects and they become absorbed into our spirit. Sometimes they release cognitive understanding but mostly our spirit receives revelation that operates from their light.

I spent many hours joyfully exploring the river flowing up and down, wherever my thoughts took me, and then one day I saw to the right a series of waterfalls. I was drawn to them, and as I thought that, the desire took me there instantly. I stood under the flow. It contained light and sound and frequency, emotions and fragrances. It was there I discovered where deep calls to deep within the sound of the waterfall (Psalm 42:7). My experiences in those waterfalls were exhilarating, with an overwhelming sense of destiny. The first time I went up that waterfall, following the desire to explore, my mind was a limitation. I could not get over the concept of going up, against the flow, and one of my angels had to lift me up. But eventually I was able to float up and down as I wished until it became a pathway and accessible by desire and thought. On one occasion I discovered a cave behind the waterfall. There were many alcoves and a man that I later found out was Enoch. As I approached him he spoke to me and gave me what he called a quest. I have met him a number of times and he always seems to be giving me various assignments.

As I followed the river up and beyond the waterfall, there was a path winding its way alongside the river. Everything is living, bursting with vibrant energy and emotions, even the paths that you walk on. This path wound through amazing beautiful trees and plants bursting with colours, vibrant beyond earthly reality. As I followed the path it led to a bridge (as I shared in another thread) but the river continues to another series of waterfalls, all cascading down into a deep pool. When I first discovered this my focus was on discovering its source so I went up the nearest waterfall and continued following the river until it came to the tree of life. It was the most amazing sight, where the river and tree merge and the river flows through it but the tree is on both sides of the river. There were leaves that were scrolls floating and they are for the healing of the nations. You can take and eat those scrolls and they authorise you to bring healing to your assigned nations. As the tree of life got closer, the river became more viscose and crystalline. I approached the tree. It was immense and transcendent but at the same time immanent and accessible. I was drawn to the amazing fruit of all shapes, sizes and colours. I took a purple fruit and as I bit into it there was an explosion of taste but also of overwhelming joy. I kept returning there, eating the scrolls and tasting the fruit whenever I felt led.

One day I had the desire to go beyond and walked right through the tree and continued in the river until it came to a huge throne with the river flowing from it. As I approached the throne I became aware of a presence that I could not see until the Father reached down and lifted me gently onto His lap. I rested my head on His chest and felt the comforting rhythm of His heart beating. I felt totally at rest, safe and secure in His arms of love at the throne of grace. I felt the need to share my deepest needs and desires and I was to discover that the more I rested the more He was working on my behalf. The grace and mercy to help meet all my needs flowed from the deepest place of rest touching the heart of the Father.

For most of us, the throne of grace was just where we would go and pray. We asked God to hear our prayer, and hopefully He would. I found that there is an actual throne of grace, a real but spiritual place that you can go and encounter. You can be completely at rest and in peace and enjoying all the help of grace and mercy you need in any situation of life because you are trusting not working.

I have had some really interesting things happen when I have been with local leaders and groups. One time we were singing songs about going to the throne of grace. People sing a lot of songs that don't mean anything to them because they have never actually engaged in the reality of what they are singing about. I challenged them to actually do that. I said "Let's go to the throne of grace". They were all just getting ready to pray, so I explained, "We are not going to pray, we are going to go to the throne of grace. Heaven is open; we've been invited to come boldly, confidently, so let's go". They looked at me as if I were mad. I said "This is how you do it". So we went. Not all of them came; some of them were just not going to do that because they did not believe you could do it, that you must be crazy if you thought you could. Others did, and they actually had an experience, which has led them to more and more experiences.

I encourage you to engage people who struggle with these things. Find a scripture that they use all the time in a completely theoretical or metaphorical context and make it real for them. Give them the reality of it by opening up the truth in personal experience and encounter because having one encounter will change people's hearts and minds more than a hundred sermons. If you can help someone have one encounter, it will change their own perception and they will want more.

On another occasion, I went into the Father's garden and sensed an even deeper level of peace. I began to rest and I began to float, not touching anything, just suspended in the atmosphere of peace and rest. The experience was of being completely at one with the Father, just intimate, loved. Then it felt like I just exploded, as if every atom of my being just dispersed out into the whole of creation. I felt connected to everything as part of a once harmonious whole. I felt and sensed the desire of creation to be made whole again. It is still something I feel today. The experience has given me a desire to respond to creation's groan for freedom as a son, to bring it back into harmony, because I felt what it was like to be in harmony with everything and what everything would be like if it were in harmony with God as He originally intended.

Those experiences opened a deeper understanding that changed my perspective of everything. The garden was wonderful. I found a pool in Father's garden which led me into His heart. I found many different routes to places and diverse ways of engaging. I found pools, rivers and waterfalls which led me into places but other people find different ways to those same places because God relates to us in a way that we can understand. Heaven is very different for individual people. This is why I don't try and describe it too much, so that everyone can experience it in their own way, having their own personal encounters so that they can be real for them.

When I enter into these supernatural encounters, most of the time I just let my spirit lead me, unless God takes me somewhere specifically. I instinctively know where to and what to engage with. I used to go to places out of inquisitiveness: I wanted to know everything, how things worked, where they were. I do not any more. My soul no longer leads me to do that. My spirit now directs me and my soul no longer needs to know. The story of how that came about is in another thread.

There is always something deeper about God. In every encounter I have ever had, there have been layers of depth. So when I have gone back into it, it has taken me deeper. So never be satisfied with one encounter, always go back. In some of the encounters I have had, I have been so awestruck with what I was experiencing that I have not looked and observed everything that was going on. By going back you can catch some of what you missed the first time! I now journal everything I see and hear, then I can always go back and keep on going back until more revelation unfolds.

When I encountered the pool with the chest, I returned there a number of times but then I found a tunnel and a corridor that took me to a dimension that I never knew existed.

The new dimension I discovered was an access into 'what was, before there was anything' (commonly called 'eternity') and there I engaged the heart of God. It is where we were created. It is the womb of His thoughts that framed our existence, where our spirit was framed. Once you see that it changes everything because then you have to be like that. That's who you are. You want to do everything possible to be who He created you to be. There are so many experiences like that.

When you are there, everything is 'now' so it is very difficult to engage cognitively with linear thinking. I stopped trying to understand those experiences and just let my spirit engage them. Many times I have found myself saying things that I do not know in my mind but which my spirit has received during those times.

Breathe

When we were created, God created us with the breath of God in us. So we were supposed to breathe it out and then breathe it in, breathe it in and breathe it out: that's the rhythm of life, 'Yod Hei Vav Hei', the name of God, His life within us.

We breathe out to frame the world by what we say. We name things according to the name of God. We breathe in and breathe out and breathe in. There is a constant flow of life that's supposed to be the rhythm of life for us. Everyone needs to breathe in from the face to face relationship we can have with God.

In the womb a baby's lungs are filled with fluid, but Adam was not created that way. He was created and God breathed into him and then Adam spoke it out. That's why he was able to shape the animals. He formed the animals and he named them. God just brought him the raw materials and the creativity to frame it. We can learn how to frame things in our own life.

This taught me that we need to become spirit beings before we engage in spirit doings. Don't be focused on what you are doing. Be focused on being and everything will flow out of your identity. Now I spend more time engaging in intimacy and allow that intimacy to direct me.

Relationship and responsibility

I discovered that there are two main pathways to engage and enter heaven. There is the pathway of relationship, which is all about intimacy with the presence and person of God, and the pathway of responsibility, which is about the position of governmental sonship.

The relationship is really important but it is vital that we don't just stay enjoying the relationship and never take responsibility. I have gone beyond hearing and seeing in the spirit to being in the spirit, so now I can live in those dual realms of heaven and earth and flow from one to the other. Jesus lived His life this way, which enabled Him always to do what He saw and heard the Father doing and saying.

And no one hath gone up to the heaven, except he who out of the heaven came down -- the Son of Man who is in the heaven (John 3:13 YLT).

No one has gone up into heaven, but there is One who came down from heaven, the Son of Man [Himself—whose home is in heaven] (John 3:13 AMP).

Relationship with our Father as sons leads us to the responsibility that operates where we are seated with Christ in the heavenly places. I will describe in another thread how this developed into multidimensional living in the heavenly spiritual realms.

Some people want that responsibility without the relationship and it doesn't work. Even more people want the relationship without the responsibility. That does not work either, we can't just 'soak' for the rest of our lives.

You have to take responsibility to seek first the kingdom and the government of God from heaven as a son. A son is a joint heir. An heir of God, therefore, has authority in the Kingdom, to administer the Kingdom on God's behalf. That is a whole different ballgame. I have learned more about being a son and what that means in the last few years than I did in my entire life. We are a heavenly royal priesthood but we must be priests before we can truly be kings. We need the relationship to be able to operate in the responsibility.

Many people are fearful of operating in responsibility because they have a wrong view of God. An example of this is described in the parable of the talents:

"And the one also who had received the one talent came up and said, 'Master, I knew you to be a hard man, reaping where you did not sow and gathering where you scattered no seed. And I was afraid, and went away and hid your talent in the ground. See, you have what is yours.'"(Matthew 25:24-25 NASB).

"The servant given one thousand said, 'Master, I know you have high standards and hate careless ways, that you demand the best and make no allowances for error. I was afraid I might disappoint you, so I found a good hiding place and secured your money. Here it is, safe and sound down to the last cent.'" (Matthew 25:24-25 TM).

Many people are failing to realise their sonship because of this wrong view of God and are not functioning as lords and kings in their heavenly positions of responsibility. We need not fear: Jesus' yoke is easy and His burden is light.

I discovered that there are many rooms in the mountain of God and different places of government. There are many thrones where God dwells and many thrones where we can be seated. There is the throne of the Ancient of Days, by the fire stones. There is the throne in the temple, where the train of His robe fills the temple. There is the mercy seat, where the presence of God manifests as the four faces of God. Then there is the throne room, where we get the lightnings and thunders, the four living creatures and the 24 elders. It is a different place because there are different functions in heaven. Until you go there and look and see what they do, then you may just think that there is just 'the throne' in heaven. God has thrones that are mobile and He moves - quite often - to different places.

Fire stones revisited

I have been back to the fire stones. It took me about three years to go back there, I didn't really think that I could. People kept asking me about it, so eventually I took a group there in a hangout online. It was a very intense place; I felt wrecked and overwhelmed and those that I helped engage were also wrecked. I realised that this happened because I didn't have the mandate to take them with me, so I had to apologise to them afterwards. Please don't go there if you are not ready.

The reason it is a really intense place is that the revelation of our purpose - mankind's purpose - and your destiny are there. When I went back to the fire stones I assumed that it was just going to be more of what I experienced the first time. So I stepped onto the first stone thinking I would engage love like before, but it was different. It took me to another level of authority. It opened up a whole realm of heavenly government that I had never experienced before.

In a subsequent fire stones encounter I was given a seal by Wisdom. The seal opened up access to different places for which there were new protocols to learn, for example in the Chancellor's Court.

I have been back a number of times and it is always deeper. The last time I went there I disappeared into each stone; I was completely absorbed into it. I have never been the same since. That encounter opened up a new dimension of heavenly realm encounters that I never even knew existed. It took me nine months to get to a point where I could talk about it. People sometimes push my buttons in the hangouts online and I try to share but sometimes I find I waffle because I cannot express what I want to say in words that make any sense. An example would be the 12 High Chancellor's houses and the circle of the deep, with all its implications for aligning 'what was' with 'what is' to release 'what will be' to be aligned with 'what was'.

We will start to discover the deeper aspects of our destiny, linked to who we were (before we were here in this dimension) and therefore who we will be again. We will find that we have a role to play as a son in the wider aspects of the restoration of all things within the order of creation. I had no idea of any of these revelations when I began my journey. I know some of you who are reading this will think, "We have no idea either" but you learn by keeping on going back into the heavenly realms and experiencing intimacy with the Father.

If you desire intimacy, if your heart is set on it, then that desire will be fulfilled. Creating a desire in our heart is another subject but if you pursue creating and cultivating desire, then everything I have been sharing becomes possible for everyone.

The fire stones in God's garden in Eden are an intense place of revelation concerning our sonship. If you get the love, joy and peace dimension, lap it up, enjoy it because it gets deeper and deeper and then you will be given more responsibility. I was not ready for the responsibility either. I am not sure I should have gone back so many times, yet I did because (once I got the mandate to do so) I was taking other people there.

I am not saying I regret it, but after the third or fourth time I would just stand back and observe other people rather than engaging there again myself. The thing is that if you engage there then you become responsible for what you have seen. I was given some positions of responsibility as a result of the times I did engage, so now I have to pursue what I am responsible for.

For example, engaging the Council of 70 came out of this experience. I was not really sure I wanted to. I was taken there to see it but the first time I went I actually couldn't even see, it was so bright. It was a totally different atmosphere; at first I struggled to even breathe there. God said, "I want you to present a case before this council for the Joshua Generation for judgment against the Moses Generation and you need to do it on the 35th day of the first session." I spent time preparing that case based on the precepts, statutes and laws of God. I presented the case on day 35 and then spent the next 35 days administrating the verdict. I thought I was finished and then God asked me to present three other cases, one for justice, one for grace and one for mercy.

I am really looking forward to the grace and mercy as I found the case for judgment really hard work. To prepare that case I needed to engage all the Chancellor's houses and understand how they worked. It took me nine months. Every time I went in there, I could not understand anything I was seeing. Some of it was just so deep I did not have the words to express what I saw but my spirit was absorbing the revelation. I kept going back as I had a deadline to get the case prepared and I needed to figure out how to do this. I sought Wisdom and Prudence for help and I did cognitively understand some of what I engaged in the High Chancellor's houses. A little of what I experienced I have now been able to explain and I know how the alignment of the 12 houses functions within the first cycle of the circle of the deep.

We have a responsibility as sons to find out about our identity and our positions of authority to be involved with ruling the house and having charge of the courts of heaven; so we can be involved in the assemblies of heaven.

Thus says the Lord of hosts, 'If you will walk in My ways and if you will perform My service, then you will also govern My house and also have charge of My courts, and I will grant you free access among these who are standing here' (Zechariah 3:7).

Romans 8:19 reveals that the whole of creation is waiting for the manifestation of the sons of God. Then it goes on to say in verse 21 that creation itself will be brought into the freedom of the glory of the children of God.

Even now, with all the things I have seen, that just amazes me. Because it's not God's glory that creation will come into, but the glory of the children of God. We will reflect God's glory by radiating that glory from ourselves, as sons who are transfigured. So we need to learn how to be transfigured, transformed, metamorphosed, which is the process I write about in the next thread.

Anyone can learn how to engage their positions in the heavenlies. I am not any more special than anyone else. We are all special; we are all God's children and He treats us all individually and uniquely. We are all created with a plan, a purpose and a destiny. Anyone can learn to do the equivalent of any of the things I have done. They may not be identical to my experiences, but you can certainly do the things you are called to do in the realms of heaven. You can learn how to rule, how to administer, present judicial cases, operate the court system. We can all learn how to do those governmental, legislative things if we flow from a place of face to face, heart to heart intimacy, where we know God as Father and see ourselves reflected in the mirror of His face.

I can teach you what I know but you can go and discover more and then teach me some of the numerous things that I don't know. I love it when people share their testimonies of encounters that I have never had; it encourages me to go and have a look for myself. Once I know that something else exists, I can access it. If you don't know something exists, you cannot go there unless you are taken. That is why explorers and forerunners are key to opening up the realms of heaven for others to follow.

People's testimonies can become a doorway to walk through. Sometimes God will just take you involuntarily and show you things because you need to know. If you are open and have a desire in your heart; you can ask the Father and He will take you to see things as a son. Wisdom will take you to places and show you protocols. I have a desire to fulfil my destiny and my spirit directed me to engage out of desire. When I first began engaging legislatively it was not because I chose to do it. I was led by my spirit so I just found myself in the Court of Kings where I instinctively began legislating something, producing a law, and then following the process through.

So having legislated and produced a law, I now know how to do it and that means I can teach other people how to do it for themselves. I am still led to legislate but now I have more insight and am more strategic in what I am mandated to do. In our church, many people legislate. On the one hand, this is great because it allows me to continue to explore new places and pioneer new things. On the other hand, it is frustrating that I don't get to do a lot of those things consistently myself.

I get to teach other people how to do them because that is my role and then God takes me onto something new.

Beyond Separating and Reintegrating Soul and Spirit

My journey of transformation beyond the dark cloud

And although you were formerly alienated and hostile in mind, engaged in evil deeds, yet He has now reconciled you in His fleshly body through death, in order to present you before Him holy and blameless and beyond reproach (Colossians 1:21-22 NASB).

Your indifferent mindset alienated you from God into a lifestyle of annoyances, hardships, and labors. Yet he has now fully reconciled and restored you to your original design. He accomplished this in dying our death in a human body; he fully represented us in order to fully present us again in blameless innocence, face-to-face with God; with no sense of guilt, suspicion, regret, or accusation; all charges against us are officially cancelled (Colossians 1:21-22 Mirror).

For as he thinks within himself [his heart], so he is (Proverbs 23:7).

We are all born with a broken, fallen mindset, believing we are separated and alienated from God. This mindset is further impacted by the world in which we live. We are influenced mostly by those around us, the significant people in our lives. I had no idea about the nature of my soul but fortunately God had created my spirit and soul for a redemptive purpose and He knows everything about me. God shaped my soul redemptively with a prophet-teacher redemptive gift set (Arthur Burk does great teaching on this subject). I am primarily wired to engage the world around me through that paradigm. I want to know how things work so that I can explain it to others. When I was a child everything was an adventure of exploration. I wanted to know how everything worked, often to the chagrin of my mother, when I took things apart and sometimes could not put them back together again. I was inquisitive, with a sense of wonder at creation and the natural world around me. I would go exploring, often coming back with an assortment of creatures that would become part of my personal zoo.

This was the background on which my identity was based, but the world has (and in particular, people have) a way of disrupting and distorting our identity whereby we lose our sense of wonder, direction and purpose. The fathering I received was less than ideal, as I shared in detail in the first thread, and as a result my identity as a son of God rather fell by the wayside.

I was driven by my need for acceptance and love to engage in relationships that were self-centred, dependent and destructive. Those relationships distorted rather than enhanced my identity; until I no longer knew who I was apart from by reference to someone else. Even when I entered into a relationship with God it was for selfish motives, about saving me from something negative, not for the positives. My relationship with Jesus as Lord was non-relational as that was the model I grew up with. As I began to enter into deeper relationships more damage was done to my emotions and therefore my self-image. The hurt that I suffered and caused in those relationships established surface behaviour patterns that masked a deep, underlying need for identity. In my teens, having been deeply hurt I vowed not to be hurt again, which set up my defence and coping mechanisms. I learned to protect myself from further hurt by mentally packaging away experiences into neat and tidy boxes in my mind and not dealing with them.

All through my formative years I was around Christianity, first in the Methodist and then the Brethren Church. These were highly evangelical environments that suited my need to understand the Bible and hold dogmatic theological and doctrinal positions. I was a searcher for truth and loved studying the Bible for principles and concepts but had no idea it was intended to lead me into a real relationship with the One who inspired it. Like most of us, I absorbed from the cultures in which I engaged the most. For me, that was the Christian and scientific cultures. I did not know it at the time, but later I realised that it shaped significantly how I perceived and interpreted the world around me.

After I was baptised in the Spirit around 1986 things began to change in many ways. My emotions began to open and my experience with God became more relational and emotional. My spirit, which previously had been very subservient to my soul, began to be edified and grew stronger until it was wrestling with my soul for control. Spiritual gifts started to emerge, particularly prophecy and distinguishing of spirits. I began to get prophetic pictures and became more sensitive to the spiritual leading, both from my own spirit and from the Holy Spirit.

For the mind set on the flesh is death, but the mind set on the Spirit is life and peace, because the mind set on the flesh is hostile toward God... For all who are being led by the Spirit of God, these are sons of God (Romans 8:6-7a, 14).

During my late teens, I discovered a book by Watchman Nee called *The Normal Christian Life* which unveiled the possibility of living free from the battle between soul and spirit. This was where I first encountered the principle of being co-crucified with Christ which was to be a recurring theme throughout my journey.

I have been crucified with Christ; and it is no longer I who live, but Christ lives in me; and the life which I now live in the flesh I live by the faith of the Son of God, who loved me and gave Himself up for me (Galatians 2:20 NASB).

The terms, co-crucified and co-alive define me now. Christ in me and I in him! (Jn 14:20). His sacrificial love is evidence of his persuasion of my righteousness! (The life that I now live in the flesh I live by the faith of the Son of God. He believes in my innocence!) (Galatians 2:20 MIR).

Later I read his much heavier tome *The Spiritual Man* which gave me my first real inkling about the nature of the soul and its need for healing and restoration.

After I was baptised in the spirit I discovered that there was healing both for my body and for my soul. Eventually, when my emotions began to surface, I realised that my mental packaging of issues did nothing but bury them within my soul. As I have explained, inner healing for me started with dealing with the issues with my father and then through the many relational issues in life; including multiple instances of betrayal from those close to me. I discovered the principle of sowing and reaping in regard to bitter root judgments. I had judged those friends who had betrayed me when I was twelve and for forty years I was still reaping the reward. I always felt alone to a degree, even in a room of people. My wounds kept my heart guarded and protected but of course that became a prison of isolation. This was only finally resolved during my encounters in heaven in 2010 when Jesus healed those betrayal wounds too.

The real key to transformation was discovering the principle of 'Forgive and Release' from the parable of the unforgiving servant in Matthew 18. This truth was a revelation that came via Joff Day[1], a friend in the church we had planted. It has become a foundational principle according to which I now live. My first forays into forgiving and releasing began with my father then extended to every area of my life.

I discovered that these were the main sources for my behavioural issues:

- Trauma – experiential programming
- Nurture – environmental programming
- Nature – genetic DNA cell memory programming

The soil of insecurity provides the perfect medium for those roots to grow. In the soil of insecurity, seeds of offence grow into roots of bitterness and produce the fruit of resentment.

The soil of insecurity arises because of a lack of love, acceptance, affirmation, approval or encouragement in our upbringing. We all have an insecure soil to some extent. Seeds of offence may be sins or things said or done – or indeed things not said or done – sown into that insecure soil.

At that point, we have an opportunity to deal with it before it has a chance to take root. If instead of removing the seed straight away, we leave it to germinate, then it quickly sends down those roots. The roots in our lives are the things that we think and feel, our responses, emotions and attitudes which develop as a result of tolerating that seed of offence sown into the insecure soil.

Then eventually, the plant will grow up and produce fruit: the things we say and the things we do, our behaviour, all as a result of the roots which have developed. When we see something happening on the surface, it is an indication that there are things going on underneath that we need to deal with. The areas in my soul that needed transforming had been sown into an insecure heart.

Seeds of offence

For example, if we begin to nurture anger because of what someone has done, that will trigger a response in our subconscious mind. We will begin to say and do things out of the roots of bitterness, producing the fruit of resentment. Reason filters kick in, distorting our view of everything, feeding our anger and resentment and causing us to make poor choices.

If someone rejects us, seeds of rejection are sown into our life. A root develops because of the hurt and pain and produces the fruit of protection. That may take the form of rejecting others first and becoming prickly or doing the opposite and becoming a doormat, accommodating people and being overly compliant, making sure we never do anything to cause anyone to reject us. Still, we feel rejected even when we are not actually being rejected because we see through that filter.

Injustice may be a seed of offence: 'it's not fair'. Life does not always treat us well. If we allow roots of self-pity (poor me) or self-hatred (I deserve it) to develop, it produces the fruit of depression, which is anger turned in on ourselves. And a victim mentality creates an environment in which unfair things happen.

When lack, poverty and deprivation are the seed of offence, the root of independence may develop, producing the fruit of self-sufficiency on the one hand and a lack of generosity on the other. Alternatively, a root of hopelessness may develop producing the fruit of failure.

One seed I found operating in me was the seed of false accusation. That produced the roots of pride ('I'm in the right') and the fruit of self-righteousness.

In all these cases, very often we simply try to remove the fruit, try to change our behaviour. Every time we cut off the fruit, though, it keeps growing back. One day, we might realise that we need also to deal with the roots, but even they will keep growing back.

We have to deal first with the original seed of offence. As long as it remains in place, attacking the fruit or the root will not have lasting success. Once the seed of offence is dealt with, we can remove the fruit and the roots without them growing back. This works for our own lives, and even for the roots of iniquity in our past generations.

Forgive and release

Most Christians know that they should forgive people but most do not know that they have to settle accounts and release the outstanding debt. They say the words "I forgive" but they don't actually forgive from the heart, so they still feel as if they are in the torture chamber. Many people don't even realise that they are hurt or holding on to an offence and therefore go on living with the consequences of other people's behaviour towards them.

Here is an example to illustrate the principle of how it works: I lend someone £100 on the basis that they will pay it back to me the next week. The time comes and goes and still no money; so when I see that person I feel owed. A seed of offence has lodged in my heart. If I let that seed stay and water and nurture it with my anger towards the person, it begins to put down roots of bitterness into my heart and eventually will produce the fruit of resentment in my life. The person avoids me so when I think of them I feel angry, bitter or resentful towards them because I have been offended and they owe me money. When I eventually catch up with them, they make excuses about why they can't pay and give assurances that they will pay it back.

I now have two different forgiveness options. First, I can choose just to forgive them for the original offence, not paying back the money. In this case they still owe me the money, and have not yet paid it back. The debt is still outstanding and I may still feel resentful because I have a seed of offence that is producing anger in me and distorts how I feel about that person. The second option is to forgive and release them. I forgive them for the original offence of not paying back the money when they said they would but, critically, I also release them from the debt: the debt is cancelled and they no longer owe me anything. I now have no right to hold anything against them, so God can heal and restore any wounds and the damage of the offence can be removed.

So many Christians go around forgiving people over and over thinking that they are following Jesus' teaching to forgive 70 x

7 times, which is 490 times (by which he meant unlimited times). Jesus never intended us to forgive the same offence 490 times but to forgive the same person 490 times if they keep re-offending. If we release the debt there is no longer any reason to be offended. The true test of forgiveness is whether I can genuinely pray for God's blessing on that person: if I cannot it is because I have not released them.

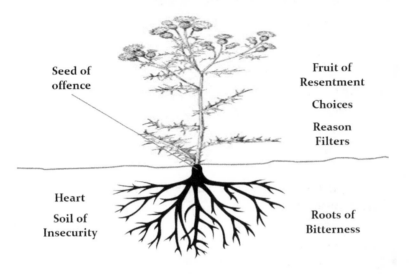

Seed of offence

Fruit of Resentment

Choices

Reason

Filters

Heart

Soil of Insecurity

Roots of Bitterness

We encourage people to make an invoice to settle the accounts as in the parable. We use a 3 column record: in column one, the offence: what was done or said (words have just as much power as actions, if not more) or what was not done or said. In column two, list what effects or consequences it has had on your life, for example in your relationships, image or identity. Then column three is how this is affecting you now, today. Once we have made the invoice and recognised the full extent of the debt owed to us, we forgive and release the person from our heart and tear up the invoice (or even burn it) as a practical expression of what we are choosing to do.

Forgive and release is a powerful preparation for inner healing or deliverance as it brings you out of the torture chamber and allows God to heal and restore your life. I have found that living a lifestyle of forgiveness stops me sleeping with the enemy and giving him a landing strip in my life. Many people keep trying to cut down the shoots and fruit that grow from the seed or try to dig up the roots but they never remove the seed of offence so roots and fruit will inevitably regrow. Below is a declaration of intent to be free.

Father, I thank you that You have made a way for me to access your heavenly presence
By your faith, I step in through the veil of Jesus through the way of the cross
I present myself to you Jesus, my High Priest, in surrender as a living sacrifice

I submit to the authority of the living Word in my life
I step through the veil of truth into the Holy Place
I stand in the light of Your truth
I ask You to search me
Reveal my blind self to me, show me the hidden motives of my heart
Show me the seeds of offence and sin that have taken root in my heart

I commit myself to forgive and release all offences in my life and my generational line
Show me all roots of bitterness that have grown in my heart
I commit myself to a lifestyle of repentance against all negative roots
I repent of all negative emotions and attitudes rooted in my heart

*Show me all fruits of resentment that have developed in my
behaviour
I commit myself to a lifestyle of renunciation of all negative
behaviours
I renounce all my defence and coping mechanisms
I renounce my sin as a way of life*

*Give me revelation of my true identity as a son of God
Give me a heart secure in its identity
Renew my mind to the mind of Christ
Meet all my unmet needs in yourself
Heal all my unhealed hurts
Restore my soul*

*I receive Your unconditional love, acceptance, affirmation, and
approval
I stand transparent, naked and unafraid before You
I hear You say "I see you and I love you"
I receive Your value, esteem and worth
I choose to live a lifestyle of forgiveness, repentance and
renunciation*

*I step back into this realm to walk in the ways of Your kingdom
Manifest Your glory through me on earth as it is in heaven
So I will fulfil my eternal destiny*

Another application of this occurred when I was popping into
my office on a day off and was accosted by someone. They
started making accusations about how I was not doing my job
properly in regard to being the chairman of trustees of one of
our charities. I felt ambushed and defensive and shocked by the
venom of the attack. My only response was "If you think you
could do a better job then go ahead". As I went home I kept

replaying the scenario in my mind wishing I had said this or that. Jesus said "Stop!" He got my attention, then He taught me a useful lesson, taking me through a process I call 'trauma to transformation'. He told me to forgive, so I forgave and released the person. That immediately removed the feelings and emotions. Then He took me through a process of reflection to identify why I was responding to the situation in the way that I did, what the trigger was to my particular reactions. Our reactions to a particular scenario could include anger, frustration, fear, passivity, defensiveness, aggression, insecurity, embarrassment etc. We usually just ignore or pass over these reactions unless they are extreme. Jesus taught me to be reflective and more sensitive to what I feel or think in any scenario.

So having chosen to forgive and release, I now looked to address my reaction. There are many ways of doing this effectively, but it must be relational and not formulaic. I evaluated my reaction: was this a godly reaction? No. You could take the reaction into a heavenly situation to reveal the roots within accusations or do a mini liebust by asking God to reveal any lies at the root of your reactions. If it is an ungodly reaction, it is essential that we own it and deal with it, and do not try to excuse or defend it. I just asked Jesus directly and He revealed different scenarios that could apply according to the circumstances.

Did this reaction reveal a weakness of character or an area of sin? If so renounce it and meditate on the Truth, Jesus, who will heal, restore and transform. If not, did this reaction reveal a weakness in skills, knowledge or understanding? If so, does God want you strong in that area? In my case, Jesus told me not to waste time trying to be stronger in an area in which I was not mandated to operate, and instead to empower someone else to operate in it by getting out of the way.

So that is what I did. I actually followed through with my offer to the person who had initially challenged me. I went to see him and told him that I was going to resign my position, so that position was open if he wanted to do it. If Jesus had told me that this was an area that I was mandated to operate in and needed to do it better, I could then have approached someone skilled in that area, humbled myself and asked for discipleship so that I could become stronger and more skilled in that area myself.

It may be that Jesus reveals that the reactions are rooted in weaknesses because of unmet needs, unhealed hurts or unresolved issues of the heart. In that case it means there are areas within our hearts which will need further investigation to discover the root cause (be it nurture, nature or trauma) and then we will need to take remedial action.

You might find the *Trauma to Transformation* flow diagrams on the next two pages helpful in working through such issues in your own life:

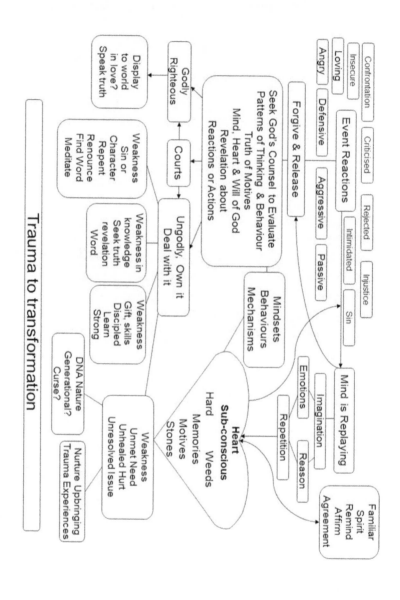

Trauma to transformation

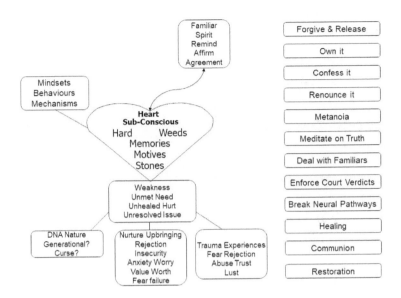

Living sacrifice

I went through a long process of what is often known as inner healing and deliverance, but that was just the preparation for deeper levels of transformation once I was able to engage with God face to face. I discovered that the more time I spent in God's presence in intimacy the more I started to become like the One I was beholding. God took me on a journey of transformation as I became a continual living sacrifice.

Therefore I urge you, brethren, by the mercies of God, to present your bodies a living and holy sacrifice, acceptable to God, which is your spiritual service of worship. And do not be conformed to this world, but be transformed by the renewing of your mind, so that you may prove what the will of God is, that which is good and acceptable and perfect (Romans 12:1-2).

I discovered that being a living sacrifice was far from easy. I began to explore the true heavenly tabernacle, the one we are invited to enter with confidence through the veil, and found what its contents symbolised to be helpful to me during the process.

Therefore, brethren, since we have confidence to enter the holy place by the blood of Jesus, by a new and living way which He inaugurated for us through the veil, that is, His flesh (Hebrews 10:19-20).

We are to lay our lives on the altar and come as a living sacrifice. That altar is not in a physical place on earth, but in the tabernacle and temple in heaven. By faith we enter through the veil, to the brazen altar, to Jesus our High Priest, who prepares the sacrifice. Our part is to come and present ourselves. Jesus told us that this is the protocol if we want to come after Him: to deny yourself (surrender), take up the cross (the place of exchange) and follow Him (Luke 9:23).

A living sacrifice is a prepared sacrifice. It will help us if we understand what was involved in offering a sacrifice in the Old Testament. When they sacrificed a lamb they prepared it in a certain way so that it was able to be received as an offering. It was the High Priest who prepared and arranged the sacrifice on the altar, and we know that Jesus is our Great High Priest (Hebrews 4:14). So now we come into the Holy Place within the heavenly tabernacle and present ourselves on the altar of incense to be a sweet-smelling aroma to God. We invite Jesus to prepare us as a sacrifice; we know what He is going to do, and we deliberately allow Him to do it.

This is how the High Priest prepared the sacrifice:

He slit its throat and drained its blood. If we are going to be prepared as a living sacrifice, we have to be willing to have our throat slit and our blood drained so that our life in the flesh is exchanged for His life in the spirit. Not literally, not physically having our throat slit, I hasten to add. But Jesus said, "You need to deny yourself, take up the cross daily, and follow me". Lose our life, to gain His life. We are going to need to totally die to doing it our way, as a choice where we say, "I die to myself, I deny myself", daily.

The head was chopped off. We cannot be in charge, with our head. Like Jesus, we have to be saying, "Not my will, but Yours be done". He is the perfect sacrifice. He did this every day. He presented Himself morning by morning as a disciple (Isaiah 50:4). I renounce the right to my free will every time my flesh gets in the way and I would choose to do what suits me rather than what suits God. Therefore "not my will but Yours be done": I am not going to let my head decide what I am going to do.

The skin was removed. We cannot have defence mechanisms, protection mechanisms and our own self-righteousness as barriers: we have to be vulnerable and transparent before God, and before others. We cannot protect ourselves: we must live in His protection. We have the armour of light, the armour of righteousness, and the armour of God to protect us. We do not have any of them if we try to protect ourselves with inferior armour of our own making. It is time to let it go.

He split the body completely open and washed all the inner parts. God wants our heart purified, refined and washed in the living water of His Word and His Presence. We have to be willing to open up our heart, open up our life. That's what a living sacrifice is, it is saying "Everything belongs to You. I am not hiding anything from You. You have it all".

Finally, he chopped the legs off. We cannot walk our own way, we have to surrender daily and walk according to how the Spirit leads. "I am going to do nothing other than what I see the Father doing" (John 5:19). That is how Jesus did His miracles: He saw the Father doing it. He is calling us to do the same: miracles, signs and wonders, being led by the Spirit daily, following Him, not doing our own thing and going off in our own direction, but every day surrendering that day to God and saying, "God, this day belongs to You. This is Your day, I surrender to your will for me as a son. You lead me, You use me, empower me, envision me, show me what You are doing".

Gateways

As I was going through this process and entering into the realms of heaven, God dwelling in me was working from the inside out. I have already described how in heaven one day I met Jacob, one of the cloud of witnesses or saints of old, and how he encouraged me to meditate on the passage in Genesis 28:12-17 about his dream of a ladder going from earth to heaven. The Lord was standing in an open door into heaven. As I meditated what really struck me was verse 17:

He was afraid and said, "How awesome is this place! This is none other than the house of God, and this is the gate of heaven."

Jacob said that this was the house of God but my mind went to my favourite chapter, John 14. The page has fallen out and been stuck back a number of times in my Bible. This chapter reveals that Jesus went to the cross to prepare us to be a house of God, "that where I am, you may be also". This was no invitation to go to heaven and live in some mansion but to be where I AM is. I AM is the relationship where Jesus is in the Father and the Father is in Him.

"If I go and prepare a place for you, I will come again and receive you to Myself, that where I am, there you may be also... Believe Me that I am in the Father and the Father is in Me... In that day you will know that I am in My Father, and you in Me, and I in you... We will come to him and make Our abode with him" (John 14:3, 11a, 20, 23).

This was an amazing revelation to me! God really did live in me but I had never personally engaged with Him there. This was a theoretical truth that was about to become an experiential truth.

It was a few days after my encounter with Jacob and my encounters with opening the door that Jesus was knocking on in my spirit that I discovered Ian Clayton's online teaching about the gateways of my spirit, soul and body.

"He who believes in Me, as the Scripture said, 'From his innermost being will flow rivers of living water.'" (John 7:38).

God has come to dwell in our innermost being. So we need to allow Him to flow through us and out of us, transforming both ourselves and the world around us.

It may be helpful over the next few pages to refer back to the image of the 'Gateways' diagram Ian received from heaven which is reproduced in the previous thread. He used it to cleanse those gateways in his own life to help facilitate being able to engage God more intimately. It took him several years to go through them all; but as I was on a 40 day fast I had a few weeks left to engage exploring and cleansing my gateways. As I described, I began going through that process to open up my life for heaven to flow through me.

Although the initial cleansing only took a few weeks I spent the next two years really getting to know myself by continuing to walk through my gateways with Jesus.

As we open the First Love Gate, the river flows out into our spirit. We surrender to the presence of God on the inside. In our spirit, there are different senses or actions of the spirit: we need to let the glory of God flow through these and activate them. It is the Holy Spirit who flows through those gates, through those doorways in our spirit, coming out into our soul.

Our spirit gates are Fear of God, Reverence, Prayer, Hope, Faith, Revelation, Intuition and Worship. And there is one more, our heavenly gate if you like. This is our access to heaven, back through that First Love Gate into the heavenly realms, following the river of life back to its source.

The first few gates are an expression of intimacy and fellowship with the presence of God in us. I began to learn how to identify and know God by experiencing who He is. I found that Father, Son and Spirit are very distinct expressions of personality, fragrance and frequency. The more time I spent embracing and hanging out with God's presence, the easier it became for me to discern the voices and language and styles of communication that the Father, Son and Spirit use.

The more I learned to fellowship, the more my level of trust increased and the deeper God was able to go in revealing the truth. This meant that when I eventually began to walk with

Jesus through my soul gates, He was able to do a deeper cleansing and purifying work.

I discovered that the other gates of my spirit were more functional and revelatory. This is where God reveals Himself through us, where we see aspects of His kingdom, where we hear His voice, where we get to see what He is doing and what He wants us to do (see John 5:19). Without the intimacy and relationship first, the other gates do not really function well.

We will all engage our gateways individually and uniquely because we are all designed by God to be special and unique. The first gates that I began to explore as Jesus walked with me were Fear of God, Reverence and Prayer. Engaging the Fear of God gate helped me understand that within me there is the all-seeing, all-knowing and omnipresent God. My revelatory experience standing in that gateway was an awesome encounter. God, who has created the universe and everything in it, has chosen to come and dwell within me and within all of us. We become a habitation and house of God because Jesus went to the cross to prepare us to be a place for Him to dwell. The all-consuming fire of God is actually dwelling inside us.

Fear of God is not the same as being afraid of Him. If I know God's love, I will not be afraid of Him. But it is an awesome experience to have Him dwell within us, and He wants us to know the awesomeness of His presence. Engaging this gateway first led naturally to the Reverence Gate. As I stood in that gate with Jesus, I had such an overwhelming desire to honour Him, to bring Him repute and glory. The thought of bringing Him dishonour or disrepute filled me with such a sense of loathing that when I engaged the Conscience Gate in my soul, it created a powerful desire which enhanced the power of my conscience to protect and direct my choices.

As I engaged the different gateways relationally, walking with Jesus and standing before, in and then going through each gate, I found that I had to let go of my preconceived ideas of what these gates meant by just interpreting the meaning of the words. My experiences were going beyond my intellectual ability to grasp. All these experiences were preparatory to my later encounters of surrendering my ego and self.

Then Jesus stood with me in my Prayer Gate. This is of course not about getting on our knees, putting our hands together, and finishing it off with 'Amen'. It is about constant two-way communication, where the Spirit of God, the mind of Christ and the heart of the Father are flowing through us relationally. That is why praying in tongues is so important: it is our spirit praying and communicating with God. And we can do that without ceasing if we train ourselves to flow continually in tongues even when our conscious mind is elsewhere. The level of communication that this gate hinted at was more of a telepathic, cardiognostic, heart to heart type knowledge and discernment. Standing there went beyond words, to frequencies, fragrances, desires and intentions.

As I engaged the Hope Gate and stood with Jesus, my dreams and destiny began to be unveiled. It was as if the scroll of my life was being written onto my heart. The essence of life flowing through this gate begins to unveil the heart behind the visions and dreams we have, until opportunities and potential for possibilities begin to form out of the creative swirl of God's thoughts towards us, activating our destiny within the context of our sonship. We can choose (and so give substance to) creative expressions of the desire and will of God which emerge from among these constantly developing possibilities.

As Jesus walked with me to my Faith Gate I was filled with expectancy and as I stood there, I already believed all that 'would be' was already expressed in the substance of faith. Many emotions washed over me, all relating to agreement, harmony, concord, understanding, knowing. This was where I experienced my first glimpse of living in the moment of the 'now' of God's mind, engaging the 'what was before there was' as it is now materialising into 'what is' and expanding into the formation of 'what will be'.

After this mind-expanding and consciousness-altering encounter, standing in the Revelation Gate and seeing inspiration, light, counsel, wisdom, intuition, gut instinct and knowing flow past me, as the Holy Spirit revealed the Father's heart to me, seemed almost an anticlimactic normality. But of course it was awesome compared to my experience of normal everyday life!

Now all those gates are great, and they can all be working wonderfully, but it doesn't mean anything without one other thing; and that is worship.

As I stood with Jesus in the Worship Gate my preconceived ideas about it just faded away because in reality worship has nothing to do with singing in a meeting. Worship is a state of complete surrender and obedience to the revelation of God's heart in mystic union which is expressed on our scroll. It is complete surrender and total submission to the will of God for our lives on a daily basis. Everything else that is flowing within us will lead us to say, "God I choose to surrender myself to you". This is His desire as Father for sons to be 'joined to the

Lord and one spirit with Him' (1 Corinthians 6:17), so that we flow together in almost symbiotic harmony.

My experiences of these gateways were so foundational to the renewal of my mind that all the time I invested has yielded great dividends.

Scroll of destiny

I was engaging at the throne of grace one day and was sitting on the Father's lap. He showed me a scroll and without looking at it, I knew this was my scroll of destiny. Sitting there with my head on His breast, I felt more than saw some of the mandates that were on my scroll. I had met 6 of the 7 spirits of God during this time, all except the Spirit of the Fear of the Lord. The Father then introduced me to him and I got down from the throne, curious and inquisitive as I was then to know everything. Little did I know what was about to happen. The Spirit of the Fear of the Lord asked, "Do you want to see your scroll?" I thought I had just seen it but I just said "Yes", thinking this was going to be great. So he gave me a scroll which was the scroll of my life. This scroll is supposed to be the record of the outworking of my destiny scroll and, of course, the two should match. The scroll was sealed on the front and back with what looked like ornate clasps.

He beckoned me to enter what I can only describe as looking like the mouth of a lion; as I approached, I started to feel apprehensive and began to physically shake. I actually felt terrified! This was the scariest thing, up to that point, that I had ever encountered in my life. This was such an intense encounter, at what I later understood was the judgment seat. I felt compelled to go in, so I walked into this dark cave, following a dim passageway until I eventually came up to the consuming fire of God's love. Our God is a consuming fire and here I was standing before Him, scroll in hand.

His intense eyes of fire started to look at me from the pillar of fire, seriously, intently looking at me, penetrating my very being. I started to seriously doubt that I would live to get out of there. My mind began to race and my thinking was running out of control (your soul still thinks, even in heaven). Sometimes I think some really stupid things, but this was really not so stupid. I was truly in fear for my life.

I presented the scroll and His eyes of fire burst the seals so that the scroll could be opened and unveiled. In an instant, everything, my whole life, flashed across my mind. There was no sin, sin is not there; this has nothing to do with sin: sin has been dealt with on the cross. This is all the things I have done as a believer and the motives behind my actions. Religion may present this as sin in a sense but, actually, God doesn't see it that way. I began to be aware that God was revealing all of the gold, silver and precious stones which were on my scroll. I sensed the intense pleasure of God's heart and was comforted. The memory of many experiences and things I had done came flooding back into my mind. My egg sandwich was there as a precious stone in my journey with Him. Such steps of obedience enabled Father to release things that He longed to give me in my life.

Then I just saw everything that I have ever done as a believer and all the motives of my heart. I became aware of the figurative wood, hay and stubble, which were all the things I had done for the wrong motives, to bless me or to make me appear better, rather than for God's glory alone.

I was horrified. I felt such regret, an overwhelming sense of "I am just so sorry". Immediately I felt such a strong sense of His love. At that point, when I owned what my life had been like, I again felt the pleasure of His heart, which blessed me and yet left me confused. Then fire just exploded from His eyes consuming all the wood, hay and straw. We don't have to wait until we are dead or Jesus returns, to go before the judgment seat and get that scroll dealt with by fire. We can all go now.

I started to back out, unable to remove my gaze from the fire until I was outside. Immediately I knew that I had to go back in because the process was not completed. I realised it was because I had only done one side of the scroll. It was sealed front and back. So I gingerly walked back in and once again stood before the consuming fire. The other side of the scroll was unveiled and many things flashed across my mind. I became aware of every opportunity in my life that God had given me up to that time, and again sensed the pleasure of His heart over the gold, silver and precious stones that marked various points in my life. Then every missed opportunity came into view. All the things that God intended me to do that I had not done. These things were more wood, hay and straw, and most of them I had never even known about because I had been distracted by life itself and the way I saw myself as less than He had intended me to be.

I could see every missed opportunity in my whole life and this created some serious regret. The realisation that I had missed all those opportunities and possibilities caused a great sadness to encompass me but at that moment His love penetrated my sadness. A very specific memory transported me back in time into a scene in which I began to observe myself. He actually showed me an area of regret that I was holding onto, a time when I thought I had made a big mistake that had damaged someone else; the memory of it had affected me ever since. When I was around 14 years old there was this girl (at that time in my life there was always a girl). Here I was back in my garden, at my house with this girl who I really, really liked. She was in our youth group and she was sitting on top of the wall, looking at me and flirting with her eyes. She asked me to go out with her. Why I said "No" when I meant to say "Yes" I never did understand. The word "No" just blurted out of my mouth. Soon afterwards she started going out with someone else instead and from then on her whole life was messed up. She became involved in drugs and some other really bad stuff and got pregnant.

I had always held myself responsible. If I had said "Yes", then everything would have been different in her life. This was an area where the enemy poked me at various times in my life. It was one of those things that was a regret that I held. Now God in His amazing love and compassion showed me what would have happened if I had gone out with her: she would have been my soul mate and I would have had little desire for the things of the spirit. So God showed me that it was my spirit that said "No" at that point. He showed me the course of my life if I had actually said "Yes" and completely freed me from all the feelings of regret.

It was really a precious moment because it was God saying "I am interested in even the smallest things in your life that have had an effect on you". It changed how I looked at little things in my life that can have a big impact, how the enemy can use them and how God is interested in freeing us from those things.

Having done that, the fire of God purged my whole scroll and I come out really happy, feeling totally different. The Spirit of the Fear of the Lord took me to an amazing waterfall and told me to jump off. At this point I had been up and down a few waterfalls, so I knew I would be okay, even though I could not see the bottom.

Just be

So I jumped off this waterfall and I ended up in the Father's garden. Most people access the garden a different way, by following the river of life and the pathway that leads to a bridge. I went down this waterfall and I found myself in the garden of God for the first time. It is the most amazing place. If you want peace and you just want to be, then that's the place to go because in there you cannot do anything. The first time I tried to do a few things and I heard "Just be". I have had some amazing encounters there of what it is to just be.

I encountered the four chambers of the heart, the garden, the dance floor, soaking room, and bridal chamber. These are intimate experiences that prepare us for sonship and identity. They bring us back into the image that God created us for (see Ephesians 1:4) so that our spirit can transform our soul. We can come back into alignment with God.

The whole process is about us realising that human beings is our identity, not human doings. Then we need to understand that we are not really human at all. We are living beings, spirit beings. Knowledge apart from God is humanism. That is the pathway of the DIY tree of the knowledge of good and evil. It is about us doing or knowing things apart from God.

I don't want to know anything apart from God because that knowledge will come from the wrong source. Even if it is good, it is still from the wrong source and has a negative effect. So really, we should and can be living beings.

The first thing babies do when they are delivered is take a breath in. That is because in the womb their lungs are filled with fluid. But Adam wasn't created that way; he was created with the breath of God in him and he spoke it out. That's why he was able to create the animals. He formed the animals and he named them. God just brought him the raw materials and the creativity to frame it. We can learn how to frame things in our own life.

We are supposed to breathe out the breath of God that is in us and then breathe in, *Yod Hei Vav Hei*. There is a Yod that we breathe out to frame the world by what we say. We name things according to the name of God. We are designed to breathe out and in, out and in; a constant flow, the rhythm of life for us.

This taught me that we need to become spirit beings before we engage in spirit doings. I discovered that if I didn't focus on what I was doing but focused on just being then everything flows from the inside out. Now I spend more time engaging in intimacy and allow that intimacy to direct me in the responsibility of sonship.

I learned to allow God to direct me by daily taking Jesus' yoke upon me and letting Him lead me to the place I need to go. I am responsible for doing what I need to do there but He leads me. So relationship must always come before responsibility. Deepening intimacy is vitally important but it is equally important not to get stuck in the relationship and never develop the responsibility of sonship. Many people enjoy the soaking experiences but are less keen on the governmental responsibility to answer creation's groan as sons.

Hebrew marriage

My journey to separate and reintegrate my soul continued through a process that mirrored the Hebrew marriage. The four chambers of the heart are the four most intimate places you can engage God within yourself but they also have corresponding - even deeper - levels in the heavenly realms.

My encounters with God within followed the river of life through the garden, dance floor, soaking room and bridal chamber of my heart. Our heart is our very core, where soul and spirit are joined in the secret place of intimacy. This is where the essence of who you are personally and redemptively can come into union with your eternal self.

Psalm 23 reflected my marriage process to establish a pure love and total trust relationship. I was prepared as the bride lying in green pastures, by quiet waters, for the restoration of my soul; a table before me, my head overflowing with oil, established as the house of the Lord to dwell forever in the intimacy of the bride and groom.

"Let us rejoice and be glad and give the glory to Him, for the marriage of the Lamb has come and His bride has made herself ready." It was given to her to clothe herself in fine linen, bright and clean; for the fine linen is the righteous acts of the saints. Then he said to me, "Write, 'Blessed are those who are invited to the marriage supper of the Lamb'"... (Revelation 19:7-9).

Husbands, love your wives, just as Christ also loved the church and gave Himself up for her, so that He might sanctify her, having cleansed her by the washing of water with the word, that He might present to Himself the church in all her glory, having no spot or wrinkle or any such thing; but that she would be holy and blameless (Ephesians 5:25-27).

Or do you not know that the one who joins himself to a prostitute is one body with her? For He says, "The two shall become one flesh." But the one who joins himself to the Lord is one spirit with Him (1 Corinthians 6:16-17).

God has always desired an intimate relationship with His people that is often equated to a marriage. He has chosen relationship with people right throughout history: Adam and Eve, Enoch, Noah, Abraham, Moses, Joshua, Samuel, David, Solomon, Jesus, the disciples - all through covenant relationship.

God has suffered the heartbreak of broken relationship as mankind has been unfaithful; but He always desires restoration and reconciliation, that we come back into a level of relationship characterised by intimacy and faithfulness.

Divorce is a painful process that many today are familiar with but God has experienced this broken relationship Himself. He has been through a divorce and He knows how painful it is, and He hates what it does to relationships. God does not hate divorce because of some theological doctrine but because of the damage it does to us in our relationships with each other and with Him.

And I saw that for all the adulteries of faithless Israel, I had sent her away and given her a writ of divorce... (Jeremiah 3:8).

"For I hate divorce," says the Lord, the God of Israel... (Malachi 2:16).

God showed me that the Hebrew marriage process had various stages that were reflected in His desire for a relationship with me as a son. He is calling people to a deeper level of intimacy but that requires a complete change, a transformation (the Greek word is metamorphosis).

Shiddukhin: the father selects a bride for His son and they are betrothed (this period is also called *kiddushim*, meaning 'sanctification' or 'set apart'). I discovered that there were so many things that I could not see and did not know but were revealed during this process.

5 aspects of marriage were opened up for me:

- *Lakah*   –   garden
- *Segullah*   –   dance floor
- *Mikveh*   –   soaking room
- *Ketubah*   –   the terms of the relationship
- *Huppah*   –   bridal chamber

The first time something occurs in the Bible it sets a precedent in biblical interpretation. God invited the children of Israel to marry Him in the wilderness. They refused through lack of identity and through fear. When God appeared they had come out of Egypt but Egypt had not come out of them. Just like so many of us today, they were free but living like slaves and orphans, not knowing the true meaning of their sonship and fearful of true intimacy in a real relationship.

Look at what happened in the first proposal of marriage: there was a canopy, a house of God, a glory cloud covering and fire. The canopy is known as the *Huppah* or *Chuppah in Hebrew*, and it is where the *Ketubah* marriage contract takes place. The description of events and the language used in Exodus 19 reflect the customs of the Hebrew marriage ceremony.

So it came about on the third day, when it was morning, that there were thunder and lightning flashes and a thick cloud upon the mountain and a very loud trumpet sound so that all the people who were in the camp trembled. And Moses brought the people out of the camp to meet God, and they stood at the foot of the mountain.

Now Mount Sinai was all in smoke because the Lord descended upon it in fire; and its smoke ascended like the smoke of a furnace, and the whole mountain quaked violently. When the sound of the trumpet grew louder and louder, Moses spoke and God answered him with thunder. The Lord came down on Mount Sinai, to the top of the mountain, and Moses went up (Exodus 19:16-20).

I was drawn to spend time engaging God in the garden of my heart. Lying down in green pastures, in the place of rest and restoration, I saw God look into my eyes with a deep desire. This was the *Lakah*, the first stage of the marriage process, "I want you for my own", reflected first in God's desire for the Hebrew people:

"Then I will take you for My people, and I will be your God; and you shall know that I am the Lord your God, who brought you out from under the burdens of the Egyptians" (Exodus 6:7).

For me, this was an intense series of emotional experiences over many months, where God's desire for me was revealed as we conversed in the green pastures of the garden of my heart. I then had another series of encounters on the dance floor, representing the *Segullah*.

Segullah means 'treasured possession'. It takes *Lakah* one step further, "I don't just want to make you Mine, I want to make you the most important person in My whole life, My treasured possession".

"Now then, if you will indeed obey My voice and keep My covenant, then you shall be My own possession among all the peoples, for all the earth is Mine; and you shall be to Me a kingdom of priests and a holy nation..." (Exodus 19:5-6).

I engaged this amazing place with a chequerboard dance floor. I danced only on the white squares, not daring to venture onto the black squares until free from the soul's control. The presence of God came swirling all around me like strands of DNA: three for the Father, three for the Son and three for the Spirit. In the dance the light, fragrance and frequencies of God's character and nature were clothing me, penetrating deep within my being; the vast sum of His thoughts infiltrating my consciousness, revealing that I am His treasured possession. The truth of my identity as an eternal son was unveiled to a deeper level than I ever thought possible, creating the desire in me to engage my positions seated in the realms of heaven. The dance was intimacy personified.

All these encounters were involuntary to begin with, until desire opened up the pathways for repeated engagements.

I then began to engage the Soaking Room, which represents the *Mikveh*. *Mikveh* means "go and wash; consecrate yourself, prepare, get ready for the betrothal agreement". It was a period which began three days before the *Ketubah* was due to take place, to make sure that they would be ready.

The Lord also said to Moses, "Go to the people and consecrate them today and tomorrow, and let them wash their garments;

146

and let them be ready for the third day, for on the third day the Lord will come down on Mount Sinai in the sight of all the people" (Exodus 19:10-11).

As I lay in this place of rest it was like being washed with the sounds, perfumes and fragrances of heaven's truth. I spent many hours soaking, with the sounds and light preparing my soul for the transformation that was to come. Just like Queen Esther, we have all been called to the kingdom for a time such as this. Esther had to undergo a time of preparation before she could come before the king; so do we to enable us to come into our positions of lordship and kingship in the kingdom realms.

Now when the turn of each young lady came to go in to King Ahasuerus, after the end of her twelve months under the regulations for the women - for the days of their beautification were completed as follows: six months with oil of myrrh and six months with spices and the cosmetics for women... (Esther 2:12).

"...And who knows whether you have not attained royalty for such a time as this?" (Esther 4:14 NASB).

"...Yet who knows whether you have come to the kingdom for such a time as this?" (Esther 4:14 NKJV).

During this period I began to prepare my *Ketubah,* or marriage contract. It eventually had 68 points which would enable me to fulfil the destiny revealed to me by God in dreams, visions and encounters. Beware, though, such a contract can become performance-oriented legalism if we don't deal with our soul.

In Exodus chapter 20, what is traditionally called the 10 commandments is actually a form of *Ketubah* that God gave the children of Israel. A *Ketubah* is a marriage contract made under a *Huppah* (a covering cloud) and it is vital for our

147

relationship that we know what God's expectations are. It is equally vital to know what our expectations of God are. Normally it would be drawn up between the two parties: on one hand the bride and her father; and on the other the groom and his father. They would make an agreement, a list of terms which defined the basic boundaries of the marriage. The bride and groom could put anything they wanted in the *Ketubah*, as long as they both agreed. Once it was agreed on, that document became the rules of the marriage. If anyone broke the terms, it was called 'marital unfaithfulness'. They would sign it, then stand and face each other. The groom would say to the bride: "I go to prepare a place for you; that where I am, there you may be also". The bride would say: "When will you come back, to receive me unto yourself?" and the groom would answer, "I do not know the day or the hour, but when my father approves the wedding chamber, he will send me back to receive you unto myself."

We recognise those familiar words from John 14, and we see that Jesus was putting His death on the cross into the context of marriage. Jesus went to the cross to prepare us to be a place of His dwelling, to prepare a place for us, a marriage chamber in us. He was resurrected and came back for us so we could a have a wedding.

In our relationship with God, our focus is on fulfilling our part of the *Ketubah*. Everything we need flows out of relationship; not from dead works, trying to earn God's favour and blessing. I use my *Ketubah* to remind me of my covenant commitment in my relationship with God and to create the expectation of who God is in the new covenant. Hope enables my engagement by faith to see manifestation of heavenly blessings.

We use our *Ketubah* as a reminder of our commitment to the relationship. Love is about giving, not receiving:

God so loved... that He gave... (John 3:16).

Our *Ketubah* helps us seek first God's kingdom in love (which is the perfect expression of righteousness) so that He can provide all we need.

God does not choose us on the basis of our good works, our past performance or history but actually in spite of it:

For if while we were enemies we were reconciled to God through the death of His Son, much more, having been reconciled, we shall be saved by His life (Romans 5:10).

But God has chosen the foolish things of the world to shame the wise, and God has chosen the weak things of the world to shame the things which are strong, and the base things of the world and the despised God has chosen, the things that are not, so that He may nullify the things that are, so that no man may boast before God (1 Corinthians 1:27-29).

God's desire is a marriage relationship with us. To make a *Ketubah* we need to understand God's promises and purpose. The new covenant becomes the basis of our *Ketubah* and it needs to be made in light of our destiny scroll that was formed in God's heart and agreed with our spirit in eternity:

Your eyes have seen my unformed substance; And in Your book were all written The days that were ordained for me, When as yet there was not one of them. How precious also are Your thoughts to me, O God! How vast is the sum of them! (Psalm 139:16-17).

The more we engage God in intimacy the more of the vast sum of His thoughts about us are revealed. We find our true identity and progressive revelation of our blueprint scroll for our lives. We can also produce our *Ketubah* from that context, because *Ketubah* is about our expectations of our relationship with God and our destiny and purpose within that relationship. In relationship, we seek first His kingdom in righteousness, which means out of our first love for Him, and then all God's promises become available to us. We are in Him and in His name.

God blessed them; and God said to them, "Be fruitful and multiply, and fill the earth, and subdue it; and rule..." (Genesis 1:28).

This mandate forms the basis of our expectations. We are blessed by God so we can expect Him to empower us to succeed and prosper to the highest level. The *Ketubah* becomes the basis of our covenant exchange or trading. We trust Him by surrendering to our destiny and He provides, protects, empowers and blesses us to prosper and succeed to the highest level. What do we put in our *Ketubah*? Everything that will bring the fulfilment of our eternal destiny. The expectation of the availability of all the resources necessary to enable us to fulfil God's purpose. It then becomes the foundational truth and reality from which we live and we can frame our lives in accordance with it.

Your *Ketubah* will enable you to rule in life and not be subject to the circumstances around you. So it is really important to spend time engaging with God about your *Ketubah* and begin to formulate it so you can be joined to Him in new covenant marriage relationship.

My *Ketubah* triggered the process of my engaging the dark cloud of His presence. This dark cloud was blown in like a cold wind from the north by Winds of Change, who is one of the 4 orders of angels assigned to help the Joshua Generation to transition out of the wilderness.

Dark Cloud

From May 2011 to March 2012, I began a process and entered a period with various encounters in a dark cloud. God hides Himself for us within a dark cloud to protect us but also to draw us deeper into His presence which transforms us:

Now when the sun was going down, a deep sleep fell upon Abram; and behold, terror and great darkness fell upon him (Genesis 15:12).

...the mountain burned with fire to the very heart of the heavens: darkness, cloud and thick gloom (Deuteronomy 4:11).

He made darkness His hiding place, His canopy around Him, Darkness of waters, thick clouds of the skies. From the brightness before Him passed His thick clouds, Hailstones and coals of fire (Psalm 18:11-12).

Clouds and thick darkness surround Him; Righteousness and justice are the foundation of His throne (Psalm 97:2).

I experienced a number of encounters which were significant steps - like milestones - on my soul's journey. On 15th November 2010, I had a vision where I saw a cloud like a nebula and my scroll of destiny flashed before my eyes. In the centre was a crucial point. All things were leading up to this point in time on the scroll and all things were then flowing from this point. I saw a fire, a blue eternal flame at this point on my scroll. I had no real idea what was coming but my heart's desire was stirred and I knew it was significant.

From January to May 2011, my heart was being prepared and my desires began to deepen. If we want to come into the presence of God, the presence of His Person, we have to be willing to go through a dark cloud experience. As I say, the dark cloud is there for our protection, but with preparation we can go through it. You do not want to meet God unprepared.

On 3rd May 2011, prompted by my spirit, I asked, "Father how do I meet You in the fire and the smoke?"

The Father responded "Son, you have met Me but you have not been hungry and thirsty enough to come where I am in the thick cloud. You have held back, you have been fearful. You have not been ready to surrender everything. If you really want to come you can but you will never be then the same. You can't act the same. You must want to come above all else, you must need to come.

"You have too many encumbrances to come; they anchor you to the world. You must be willing to have them dissolved away. You have been far too comfortable. The gathering angels need to gather from you the things that hold you to the ground and restrict your range of movement. Son, I fear that if you come now you would not go back. Prepare yourself; discipline the flesh, discipline your mind. Surrender your emotions again and I will welcome you in to see Me".

On the 6th Nov 2011, during a worship time, I was lost in the presence of God on the dance floor within a swirling curtain of colour and I was instructed to spend the next 4 months in the garden, dance floor, soaking room and bridal chamber. I was to take my *Ketubah* marriage contract with me into the canopy of darkness, into the presence of the person of God, for consummation. During another encounter, the Father revealed that February 20th 2012 would be my breakthrough day.

The garden for love, the dance floor for joy, the soaking room for peace, and the bridal chamber for hope – four months of those things did not sound too bad. Remembering what had happened during my time of fasting, I was excited to begin my four months of deeper intimacy. But it turned out to be a time of darkness, in which I could do nothing, see nothing, know nothing, ultimately even be nothing, a time of intense testing.

On the first day of November 2011, I got up at 5 am looking forward to engaging God and I found I could not see anything. It was all darkness. I began to seek God for what He was doing. He told me, "I don't need your assistance, just your surrender". All He said from that point was "Be still". I knew, of course, that the scripture was from Psalm 46:10, *"Be still and know that I am God"* (NKJV) and I had had no problem being still until He said to be still. Then I lost all restraint. It was as if my spirit took a back seat and allowed my soul to be exposed. I had to know why I needed to be still, what did I need to know? Every possible question exploded from my soul with no answer but "Be still".

Redemptive gifts are the way God has wired us to connect with the world around us; they are Prophet, Servant, Teacher, Exhorter, Giver, Ruler and Mercy. Having the Prophet/Teacher redemptive gifts, I am wired by God to be inquisitive and I always wanted to know the why and how of things. I told myself that I needed to know so that I could explain it to others. What I discovered was that I needed to know because I got my identity from knowing. That was why I really needed to know, and I discovered that I only really trusted God when I knew what He was doing. Of course I thought I trusted God implicitly but when this was tested I found that my soul needed to know to be secure.

I went through the month of November frustrated and with my soul's true colours exposed. I desperately hoped that December would be better but again I could not see anything. All was darkness and all I heard was "Wait". Oh, the frustration as once again my soul exploded with questions - "What am I waiting for? Why do I need to wait?" – incessant questions for two more weeks before my soul finally gave up and I surrendered. If I had been shown an area of sin to deal with that would have been no problem, but this was the very core of my being, it was how God had wired me that I needed to surrender. I no longer needed to know anything and I questioned no more but waited patiently. The next month, January 2012, came and again all I heard was "Rest". This time I just rested. My soul had no more desire or energy to question or think.

This time of darkness and testing answered the questions that my soul could not have answered truthfully. Would I trust God without seeing and knowing what He was doing? Could joy come from nothing external, only from relationship? Was I willing to take the yoke of Jesus, to offer my obedience even when it made no sense?

In the fourth month, February 2012, in the bridal chamber, I was instructed to wait expectantly in hope. My *Ketubah* which had been the trigger for this process came to my mind. I suddenly realised how performance-orientated this could have been with my soul as it used to be. It could have been like bringing out marriage vows each morning and reminding your partner of their obligations. Just as marriage is not about the other person's obligations, but about our desire to be the best husband or wife we can be, so too with our relationship with God. We need to rest in our identity of sonship, both relationally and in responsibility and trust that God will be the Father we need to enable us to fulfil our destiny.

I decided to burn my *Ketubah* as an offering to God on the first day of February 2012 and I then entered into 21 days of fasting. I spent the first six days reviewing 15 months of my journals, waiting expectantly (which is another way of saying that I was at the end of my tether).

I had not been ill for 16 years, but I became sick by drinking contaminated water because I had not cleaned out the water cooler properly. I had no sleep for 5 days, could not even keep water down, and was physically running on empty, all reserves gone. I did not do what I would advise anyone else to do, I did not fight, stand against the sickness, or call the elders – God said just to wait so I waited as expectantly as I could.

I started to lose my reasoning abilities, I could not focus, was struggling even to pray in tongues. Emotionally I started to feel really vulnerable: I felt like I was dying and needed to put my house in order. I began to think that nobody at home would miss me if I wasn't around. I realised I had sown 18 years of my life into church to the detriment of my relationships with my wife and family, that my priorities needed to change.

I wondered if I would make it to February 20th, my breakthrough day.

I began to meditate on Psalms 22 and 42 and began to identify with the intensity of the emotions expressed by the psalmist in the separation of his soul.

My God, my God, why have You forsaken me? Far from my deliverance are the words of my groaning. O my God, I cry by day, but You do not answer; And by night, but I have no rest. Yet You are holy, O You who are enthroned upon the praises of Israel... Be not far from me, for trouble is near; For there is none to help. Many bulls have surrounded me; Strong bulls of Bashan have encircled me. They open wide their mouth at me, As a ravening and a roaring lion. I am poured out like water; My heart is like wax; It is melted within me. My strength is dried up like a potsherd, And my tongue cleaves to my jaws; And You lay me in the dust of death (Psalm 22:1-3, 11-15).

Physically I was totally empty and my soul was crying out during the separation process. Mentally I started losing my reasoning abilities. I could not focus so much so that I was struggling to pray, even in tongues.

As the deer pants for the water brooks, So my soul pants for You, O God. My soul thirsts for God, for the living God; When shall I come and appear before God? My tears have been my food day and night, While they say to me all day long, "Where is your God?" These things I remember and I pour out my soul within me... Why are you in despair, O my soul? And why have you become disturbed within me? Hope in God, for I shall again praise Him For the help of His presence. O my God, my soul is in despair within me... All Your breakers and Your waves have rolled over me.... I will say to God my rock, "Why have You forgotten me? Why do I go mourning because of the oppression...?" (Psalm 42:1-7, 9).

156

Over the next few weeks, I felt intense fire inside and out, waves of loss were rolling over me: disappointment, despair, despondency, grief. The 68 points of the marriage contract which I had drawn up in obedience to what God had told me were lost one by one. It was like each one of my dreams, visions and expectations died and I really grieved over each one. I had feelings of disappointment, loss, despair, despondency and grief.

What He was asking was "Do you still trust and love me if...?"

If none of your dreams were realised?
If none of the prophecies will come to pass?
If your destiny is never fulfilled?

I began then to seriously question myself:

Would I still love God?
Would I still trust God?
Would I still have joy and peace?
Would I still be able to rejoice and give thanks?
Would God still be a good God to me?
Could God trust me?
Was it all about Him? Or was it about me?
Was it about what He could do for me?
Was it about what I could do for Him?

God was testing my heart motives. He was refining and purifying my heart because the pure in heart will see God. God wanted me to meet Him face to face. Why? Because He loves me! And He wanted to restore me to original condition. He wanted to give me the fullness of His blessing so I could find my heavenly identity and position as a son. He wanted to release me into the fullness of authority as a son but my soul would not allow it. I was operating independently but now with my soul and spirit separated, I could be restored to wholeness. The question that I faced was:

Was it all worth it just for a relationship with Him and nothing else?

Eventually, the truth began to be revealed that the answer was YES.

"When you pass through the waters, I will be with you; And through the rivers, they will not overflow you. When you walk through the fire, you will not be scorched, Nor will the flame burn you" (Isaiah 43:2).

I now knew that if God never did another thing, I would still trust Him and love Him and if I never did another thing for Him, He would still love me. I had been crucified with Christ and now I no longer lived.

I have been crucified with Christ; and it is no longer I who live, but Christ lives in me; and the life which I now live in the flesh I live by faith in [properly *'of'*] *the Son of God, who loved me and gave Himself up for me* (Galatians 2:20).

Redemptive gifts

I mentioned that my redemptive gift is prophet/teacher, and this is how God wired me to be self-aware and to engage the physical world. I am wired to know how things work and function; to be able to explain them to others. The issue was that this gave me my identity and security. The core essence of who I was redemptively was being used to create its own identity and bring me security in independence from my spirit.

'Me, myself and I' had to surrender – soul and spirit separated – so that I could become reintegrated in oneness of spirit and soul and joined to become one spirit with God (1 Corinthians 6:17).

I believe God desires to free all His children from the need for the soul to gain identity by works, and that therefore the essence of who we are redemptively will be tested. Each person is and has a primary gift that influences the course of our lives, regardless of whether we follow or reject Christ. Psychologists term these differences in people 'basic temperaments' or 'personality types'. The redemptive gifts are received at conception, rather than salvation:

"Before I formed you in the womb I knew you, And before you were born I consecrated you; I have appointed you a prophet to the nations" (Jeremiah 1:5).

We are designed with purpose. Our redemptive gift is the grace of God woven into who we are, so that when we receive the revelation that we are made right with God we become able to honour Him with how He has made us to be.

Reintegrated

Monday 20th February came and I awoke totally restored to health and wholeness. The shackles were removed, and I was free to minister again. Straight away I could see and hear and I found I was able to engage God in the heavenlies.

But now it was different! I felt whole and integrated; my soul had died to independence but having been separated from my spirit was now whole and reintegrated. I no longer needed to know and God was free to unveil and reveal what was beyond my wildest dreams and imagination. Up to this point, my soul had not allowed my spirit to remain in the heavenly realms but suddenly, I could step in both soul and spirit, and after engaging, my spirit would remain in that realm. From that point on, my spirit has remained seated in heavenly places allowing me to flow from heaven to earth as a gateway. I can shift the focus of my consciousness to engage where I am in the heavenlies with my soul joining my spirit or I can flow quantum entangled from heaven to earth.

I eventually made it through the dark cloud and encountered the person of God. Even after all the transformation, I could spend only a microsecond looking at His amazing person. I remembered Ian Clayton saying "Don't look into His eyes" but as I gazed at one facet of His amazing face it was all too much for me, like looking at a mirror within a mirror extending into eternity.

Can God trust us, His church, with all that He desires to give us? Is God more important to us than what He does for us? In my case I could not say so without the purifying of my heart. God disciplines those He loves because He wants the best for us.

Not everyone will have to go through what I went through. I am a forerunner: I break through for others to follow. But are you willing to go through the fire of refinement, purification and preparation? Whatever this means for you, are you really willing for the motives of your heart to be tested in the fire?

Careful how you answer.

It changed me forever and opened up eternity to me. The dark cloud covering was where the essence of self needed to be yielded, surrendered. A total death to self-rule and self being in control as the principle of life took place. My soul and spirit were daily engaging heaven together; it was a visionary cognitive experience.

I had been used to stepping in through the veil and stepping back out, visiting the heavenly realm but not inhabiting and living in dual realms. I was using my soul to engage heaven to know and see what the Father was doing but my soul would not allow my spirit to engage on its own or to stay there.

This is what God desires to put into order – spirit, soul, body and world. When I became untethered from the earth, dual realms living became possible as spirit and soul became unified and connected in heaven and on earth. My spirit could stay in heaven and my soul became the channel for heaven to touch earth. Expanding the kingdom as a gateway of heaven into the earth became possible by being joined to the Lord and becoming one spirit with Him.

Now that my soul and spirit are reintegrated, I mostly just go when and where my spirit leads me. I don't go to places any more out of inquisitiveness like I once did when I wanted to know everything, how things worked, where they were and all those details. I don't do that anymore, even though with my Prophet/Teacher redemptive gift I am wired that way, because it is no longer my soul that is leading me. My spirit now directs and that is a major aspect of the ability to live in dual and multidimensional realms.

When I no longer needed to know, then God was able to reveal beyond what I could have imagined or thought possible. I went deeper into every encounter I had ever had in heaven and went to places and engaged in things I had never seen before.

Wisdom

Jesus took me to Wisdom's heights, an amazing place at the barrier or matrix between the realms of Kingdom of Heaven and Heaven, and introduced me to Wisdom, whom I had never met before. Wisdom calls to the sons of men and she helps kings, princes and nobles rule governmentally in their positions of sonship.

Does not wisdom call, And understanding lift up her voice? On top of the heights beside the way, Where the paths meet, she takes her stand; Beside the gates, at the opening to the city, At the entrance of the doors, she cries out: "To you, O men, I call, And my voice is to the sons of men...

"Counsel is mine and sound wisdom; I am understanding, power is mine. By me kings reign, And rulers decree justice. By me princes rule, and nobles, All who judge rightly. I love those who love me; And those who diligently seek me will find me".

Wisdom has built her house, She has hewn out her seven pillars; She has prepared her food, she has mixed her wine; She has also set her table; She has sent out her maidens, she calls From the tops of the heights of the city... (Proverbs 8:1-4, 14-17, 9:1-3).

Frame each day

I frame each day to succeed, with the favour and blessing of God around me. By 'frame' I mean that I prepare it in heaven so that it can be worked out on the earth through my life as a gateway of heaven. I decree, declare, call forth, release sounds, frequencies and fragrances, and I assign angels. These are the hopes or expectations that faith becomes the substance of, so that the spiritual blessings in the heavenlies mentioned in Ephesians 1:3 can be manifested. The blessings are the empowerments to prosper and succeed to the highest level attached to my identity and destiny as a son.

Therefore I am in full faith for all I need to fulfil my mandated purpose; time is framed to contract and expand around me to enable me to complete the work God has assigned me. I am therefore never too busy to do all that He desires to do through me. I have all the resources necessary available to me to enable me to subdue, solve and overcome every obstacle, problem and hindrance the enemy seeks to put in my way. I frame my day and my night so that I have all the rest my soul and body needs whilst my spirit is active in the heavenly realms. I am continually connected to heaven's creative light source which operates at a speed faster than created light. This means that everything is therefore always available first or 'before' in heaven, so I am able to have everything I am going to need ready and waiting for me whenever I need it. In that way, I can be a gateway of heaven on the earth and heaven can flow through me. My tutors and trainers for sonship, the 7 spirits of God, are actively releasing wisdom, knowledge, understanding, counsel, strength and authority from a higher and superior realm into my life.

What I believe about God and myself determines my attitude to life, therefore I am not subject to any circumstances. I am the head and not the tail: circumstances change to enable me to live in rest and peace and fulfil my daily mandates from God. As I seek first His kingdom in righteousness, I have a full expectation that He will add all that I need because I AM THAT I AM lives in me, enabling me to succeed from the perspective of God's heart in eternity. As I engage the now, the 'what was' before there was anything, and align myself in 'what is', my sonship position in heaven, I will create 'what will be' and be a history maker who aligns the beginning and end to complete the circle of the ancient pathway. I am all I need to be and possess all I need to have to be blessed and prosperous.

This is the reality of 2 Cor 9:8, that at all times in all circumstances I have all grace - God's divine enabling power - to meet all my needs and enable me to do all the God-works prepared for me, to bring glory and honour to Him. I have a full expectation of succeeding each day as my day is subject to my rule and it is not left to chance. I align my life with my scroll of destiny and not with my generational history by being a continual living sacrifice. I will be fulfilled, satisfied, content and filled with love, joy and peace.

I live according to my eternal identity and fully embrace my destiny in God's kingdom. I am the answer to creation's groan as a manifested son of God. I expect Jesus as my high priest after the order of Melchizedek to prepare me to serve Him as I as yield and surrender to His perfect will for my life each day. I accept the responsibility of sonship and my roles within His heavenly and earthly kingdom. He is my head and I accept the responsibility of His government upon my shoulders.

I daily decree and declare "Here I am, send me" so life is always an adventure. I open my heart to God daily that He would write on the tablets of my heart and unveil and reveal His will for me so that the desires of my heart will be aligned with His desires and so direct, guide and draw me towards my destiny each day. I stand daily in God's heart in eternity so that my spirit will be programmed by His thoughts about me. I stand in eternity where there is no sin to filter the light of truth that becomes my true reality, so that I can engage the revelation of His will and purpose encoded in creative light. I am in the light matrix of His creative thoughts and words which is the true fabric and essence of who I am.

Relationship and responsibility

I discovered that my dark cloud experience had produced a pathway of relationship that leads to deeper intimacy with God. Everything began flowing from the inside out; heaven flows in us and through the gateways of our spirit, soul and body to the world around us. Heaven responded to my new level of relationship by opening up the pathway of responsibility, revealing where I am seated in heavenly places in my positions of sonship. I also began to engage more interactively with the 7 Spirits of God who began to tutor me in the governmental and legislative aspects of my sonship.

I also discovered the wonderful pathway of responsibility. I discovered Zion, the mountain of God; I discovered the realm of His Kingdom and how to rule. A mountain is a governmental position in heaven, intended for each of us, where we operate in authority. I discovered my seven personal mountain spheres of government, each of which have seven sub-spheres. Individuals may have further spheres of government, depending on what they are called to do.

I discovered places of legislation, courts and assemblies of heavenly government. I discovered how to minister there, how to administer the Kingdom and how to effectively bring the rule of God from that place, so that I live on earth in the 'as it is in heaven'. This is something you really have to learn, not something you just know. You can be taught, but you have to learn how to do it. You have to learn how to use the courts of heaven and everything else in that realm.

The 7 Spirits of God directed me. I engaged with Wisdom on Wisdom's heights; she is there to help kings, princes and nobles rule in righteousness and justice, just as Proverbs 8 tells us. If you need help to understand how to rule, then Wisdom is who you need to engage with.

I struggled with that for a while because I was spending so much time with Wisdom that I wasn't spending as-much time with God. One day I asked Him "Are you okay with this?" He just smiled and said "Of course I am. I created her for that purpose".

Revelation of destiny

Part of knowing what your destiny is relates to the whole order of creation and how we are supposed to bring creation into proper order. When I was given a seal, I began to discover a new level of understanding concerning legislation. I learned about the role of a chancellor and about what I was authorised to carry out in the Chancellors' court. These encounters opened up a whole realm of heavenly revelation that I never even knew existed.

If you desire to know what you are called to do, set the desire of your heart upon it and then that desire will be fulfilled. It is important to learn how to create and cultivate God's desire in our heart.

We generally think everything is a rehash of everything that has been. But I have seen things coming that no one on earth has ever seen, things that have never been known before. They are hidden in the mysteries of darkness. God is revealing them and bringing them into light because people are engaging there now. I went into that and saw some things which I know are coming but still cannot describe.

It is like bringing someone from the 1700's into today. You try to describe an iPhone and you say, "That is what an iPhone is". They would hear the words but be unable to understand: "What is an 'i' and what is a 'phone'?" They would have no grid or reference for any of it.

Imagine 300 years of what we call 'technology', multiplied to the nth degree, and then forget about technology and think instead about the ability to make and create, to manifest from the unseen realm, rather than to build. The future will not be made of things that we build. It will be things that are created and released out of those mysteries, power sources and all sorts of amazing things that will enable us to establish embassies of heaven on the earth and rule under heaven's government on the earth. I cannot describe them to you. I have seen them. I can say 'power sources' because I know some of it was to do with that kind of concept. Beyond that, my spirit has absorbed something, but I cannot give you any words because I do not know the words - the very words do not even exist yet, they have not been released.

I am struggling even to describe a fraction of what I have seen. We are called to answer creation's groan: imagine what that will take! There is so much more out there for us to discover as we mature into manifest sonship and bring creation into the glory of the sons of God.

Legislation

As the revelation of my pre-existent eternal sonship began to be unveiled I started to spend time with Wisdom who introduced me to the courts of heaven and unveiled the protocols for producing and using legislation. She took me to the Court of Kings where I was taught how to produce and receive legislation and laws. She showed me the Court of Chancellors where legislation was authorised and sealed and the Court of Scribes where authorised legislation was written into the records and placed on the statute books.

Wisdom took me back to the fire stones beside the river of fire which flows from the throne of the Ancient of Days, and there I realised my identity and authority as a son. Wisdom gave me a Chancellor's seal and staff, introduced me to the 12 High Chancellors who opened their houses for me to engage. I also engaged an angel, Prudence, and her gifts to open the revelation of the 12 houses.

Prudence engaged me in one of our Sunday gatherings and gave me 7 gifts, telling me that they would enable me to navigate the new dimensions of the spiritual realms which were about to be opened to me. They were a sextant, compass, log books, map of territories, instruments for measuring wind (sound) and waves (light) and the trumpet to herald the call. Unknown to me, someone in the room observed what was occurring in the spirit realm and painted this picture of Prudence (opposite).

It took me 18 months exploring and investigating the High Chancellors' houses before I became aware of how they related to the Circle of the Deep and the sacred geometry of Metatron's Cube. Wisdom took me to the Court of the Councils of the Fathers where I was given the mandate to present a court case before the Council of 70. Using the revelation from my encounters with the High Chancellors' houses, I learnt to present a case based on the precepts, statutes and laws of God. In 2015, I engaged the Court of 70 in a very specific way as instructed. In February 2015, I was told to spend 35 days preparing the case for Judgment, to present on day 35 and then spend 35 days administrating and legislating the verdict that would be received. This cycle repeated throughout the year with cases for Justice, Grace and finally Mercy.

The case was produced based on the Precepts of God which describe the eternal nature and purpose of His desire.

'What was' (the eternal I AM) becomes 'what will be' and the beginning and the end meet when we bring it into 'what is' and provide kingdom government.

The judgment marks the end of the old Moses Generation order and the establishing of the new Joshua Generation, operating according to the order of Melchizedek

.

Beyond Deconstruction

Deconstruction and renewal

Another major thread of my journey involves the deconstruction and renewal of my mind.

Information we have received from birth through our senses gives us our frame of reference. Our belief systems can act as a filter in our mind. Then whatever information we receive, it is processed in such a way that it only reaffirms our existing interpretation and opinions. This is called 'confirmation bias', and causes us to habitually frame our reality from an earthly perspective rather than a heavenly one.

And do not be conformed to this world, but be transformed by the renewing of your mind, so that you may prove what the will of God is, that which is good and acceptable and perfect (Romans 12:2).

Our subconscious mind directing our conscious thinking is the key to our transformation.

For as he thinks within himself [or *in his heart*], *so he is* (Proverbs 23:7).

The natural senses receive 40 million bits of information a second, so the mind processes trillions of bits of information each day (around 40,000,000 x 86,400 = 3.456 trillion). Most of that information is shredded by an area of the brain called the hippocampus, and we store in our memory only what is important.

Anything we continually repeat gets stored as memories. These memories become the experiential programming of our reality. We become conditioned by our experiences to live from them

171

and we live by repeating those cycles of learned behaviour. Our consciousness forms neural pathways to the memories stored in our subconscious mind or heart. Some experiences, usually those which are highly traumatic or pleasurable, get immediately stored. Environmental triggers load programs into our conscious mind as thoughts and the human brain has about 100 billion neurons (or nerve cells) and many more neuroglia which serve to support and protect the neurons. Each neuron may be connected to up to 10,000 other neurons, passing signals to each other via as many as 1,000 trillion synaptic connections, equivalent by some estimates to a computer with a 1 trillion bit per second processor.

Changing our thinking is critical to being transformed. If we are going to live free, we will need to learn to use the verdict from a heavenly court to break neural pathways attached to lies and the pathways of habitual behaviour and to reconnect to the truth. Court cases in themselves are not a panacea for all problems: the verdicts given to us by our Father the judge must be applied to our minds, enabling us to take captive every thought.

We are destroying speculations and every lofty thing raised up against the knowledge of God, and we are taking every thought captive to the obedience of Christ (2 Corinthians 10:5).

Some of the thoughts we need to take captive relate to problems we may struggle with and could include: rejection, self-pity, fear, unforgiveness, fear of man, self-hatred, guilt, shame and condemnation.

Wrong thinking affects our whole being: we were created spirit, soul and body to function holistically. It can affect us emotionally and physically even to the point of causing or contributing to sickness and disease.

As thoughts grow, they become neural pathways and networks connected to the memories. Quantum physics indicates that our thoughts are designed to create our reality and that they can affect us both genetically and epigenetically. We become like that which we behold and we create our own reality by what we think about. Therefore, if we are to live in health and so fulfil our destiny, it is vitally important that we fix our eyes on Jesus, the author and completer of our faith, and focus our thinking on that which is good - and from a heavenly perspective.

Therefore if you have been raised up with Christ, keep seeking the things above, where Christ is, seated at the right hand of God. Set your mind on the things above, not on the things that are on earth (Colossians 3:1-2).

Be anxious for nothing, but in everything by prayer and supplication with thanksgiving let your requests be made known to God. And the peace of God, which surpasses all comprehension, will guard your hearts and your minds in Christ Jesus. Finally, brethren, whatever is true, whatever is honourable, whatever is right, whatever is pure, whatever is lovely, whatever is of good repute, if there is any excellence and if anything worthy of praise, dwell on these things (Philippians 4:6-8).

There are good intellectual and medical as well as spiritual reasons to forgive. Forgiveness helps to keep us mentally, emotionally and physically healthy. *A joyful heart is good medicine, But a broken spirit dries up the bones* (Proverbs 17:22).

And do not be conformed to this world, but be transformed by the renewing of your mind... (Romans 12:2).

This is the process to turn trauma into transformation. Be reflective and willing to engage your own reactions and use them as stepping stones to change.

Search me, O God, and know my heart; Try me and know my anxious thoughts; and see if there be any hurtful way in me, and lead me in the everlasting way (Psalm 139:23-24).

We can follow this process by engaging in Liebusting sessions and court cases to search, try and purify our hearts.

This process of deconstruction of the mind began for me in earnest at the beginning of 2016. As I was engaging with God, He asked me to set aside some time each day to legislate in the courts of heaven. With that mandate, I decided to spend some time each night before I went to bed to legislate (to make or enact laws) and use the authority released by these laws to provide, create, prepare or rule. I did not know where to start so I visited the Court of the Fathers to seek some guidance. The Fathers gave me some insight into various areas where legislation was needed. This gave me a larger perspective and a deeper insight into the processes of heavenly government. This is essential if we are to fulfil our mandates of sonship and answer creation's groan by participating in the restoration of all things.

I began in the Court of Kings and as I was seated there, God started to speak to me about how His children suffer from limitations and restrictions of thinking. This is what He said:

"The mists around the closed and clouded minds must be dissipated. The hindrances and entanglements must be removed, so the limitations of minds that are stuck in what has been can become free to embrace 'what can be' so it can become 'what will be'. The veils must be removed and restrictions lifted to embrace the limitless potential of My reality. The way, truth and life are to be experienced, not conceptualised and contained. The limits of what is possible must be removed for My purpose to be achieved.

"You must begin to entertain limitless grace and mercy to be able to grasp what is true reality beyond all expectations. New dimensions of everything can be yours if you are willing to let go of the old and embrace the challenge of the new."

I made a law, the Law of Deconstruction (see appendix), and I began making decrees and declarations as authorised to remove the restrictions and limitations:

> I call for the removal of the limits to unveil the beyond, the limitless potential possibilities of eternal reality.

> I call for freedom from the religious restrictions that are creating limitations.

> I call for justice against all the fear-based entanglements that are hindering the exchange.

> I call the heavenly hosts to witness for justice that all mind-sets of limitation will be exposed and removed.

> I call for the courage and boldness to possess the unknown to be instilled into our hearts and minds.

> I call for all selfishness to be exposed and surrendered.

> I call for hearts, minds and wills to be filled with compassion, zeal and passion.

I call for all confusion to be removed from hearts and minds.

I call for all obstacles to be removed from those who will be drawn to the light.

I call for the mountains to be made low and the valleys lifted up, the rough places smooth and the crooked paths made straight.

Little did I know that "Jehovah Sneaky" was about to be revealed as "Jehovah Set-up" and use my own law and decrees to iconoclastically deconstruct my conscious, subconscious and unconscious mind.

It was C. S. Lewis who called God 'the Great Iconoclast'.

This is a definition of *iconoclastic* from Dictionary.com: *Attacking or ignoring cherished beliefs and long-held traditions, etc... breaking or destroying images, especially those set up for religious veneration.*

C.S. Lewis wrote[2], *"God must continually work as the iconoclast. Every idea of Him we form He must in mercy shatter. The most blessed result of prayer would be to rise thinking, 'But I never knew before. I never dreamed...'"* (Letters to Malcolm: Chiefly on Prayer).

Again, in *The Great Divorce*, he wrote[3], *"There are three images in my mind which I must continually forsake and replace by better ones: the false image of God, the false image of my neighbours, and the false image of myself."*

My journey towards the renewal of my mind began in earnest, with God using the very legislation that I had produced - and my own decrees and declarations - to deconstruct my mind of the veils that I never even knew covered it. I discovered somewhat painfully that to be able to truly know God who is Father, Son and Spirit, and to know our identity in sonship in Him, we need to have the existing wrong frameworks in our minds deconstructed. These are our belief systems which cause or contribute to our limitations and restrictions.

Assumptions and presumptions

God began to challenge the assumptions and presumptions that I did not even know I had about Him, His values and His ways.

God can use anything to unveil our wrong assumptions: He chose voting to challenge mine in a big way. In the UK in 2016, we had a national referendum on an issue which became known as "Brexit": whether the UK should remain in or leave the European Union. It was a vitriolic fear-based campaign on both sides of the argument. To be honest I had very little time for it as everything presented, including from many considered "prophetic voices", seemed to be promoting an agenda of fear.

During this time God asked me how I was going to vote. I told Him.

[However, I am not going to tell you. For one thing it is irrelevant to the story but also I do not believe Christians should use and abuse their positions of influence to tell people which way to vote. They should come to that decision for themselves, not based on the opinions of others. Anyway, enough of the rant and back to the point of the story.]

God said "Why are going to vote that way?"

I said "Because that is the way You would want me to vote."

177

God: "When did I say that?"

Me: "Well I knew You would."

I could already tell that I was digging myself into a hole that I was not going to get out of easily.

God: "How did you know?"

I stopped digging the hole and said nothing.

God: "Did you ask me which way I wanted you to vote?"

Me: "No, I made an assumption."

God: "Ah, now we are getting to the heart of the matter!"

Trying to get off the subject, I boldly asked "Which way is the vote going to go?"

God told me and asked "Which way are you going to vote?"

Me: "The way the vote will go."

God: "Why?"

Me: "Because You want me to."

God: "Why did you assume that?"

Me: "Because that's the way You want the vote to go."

God: "Why did you assume that? You never asked Me, you presumed again."

Me (rather exasperated) "Sorry, which way do You want me to vote?"

God said "The opposite way."

Now I was completely confused. "I don't understand! You want me to vote this way, even though the vote will go the other way?"

God: "Yes."

Me: "Why?"

God: "That is My business. Why do you need to know?"

Me: "I am confused, Father"

God: "Don't allow what you think you know about Me to influence your decisions. I just want you to trust Me. I am trying to teach you to trust Me even when you don't understand, which will be often. Son, always seek Me first because I always have a bigger agenda than your assumptions. I always see a bigger picture than you can imagine. I am asking you to vote against what will be the outcome because I want to teach you how to respond afterwards. I am not partisan; I don't support any political party above another. My will for the outcome does not mean that I validate any political agenda. I always have a higher agenda and purpose than the opinions of men."

This is interesting, because I connected with a lot of people in the USA with regard to the presidential election in 2016 which saw Donald Trump elected. How many of those who were on the losing side of the vote are now not behaving in a godly way or seeing the bigger picture? And how many of those who were on the winning side of the vote think that God has validated their political view and are also now not behaving in a godly way or seeing the bigger picture?

God was not finished with me yet! He wanted me to realise how many assumptions I habitually made about Him and how that led to my presumptive choices. He asked me why I usually voted in elections in the way I did.

I had not learned my lesson. "Because You want me to."

God "Oh. When did I tell you that?"

Me: "Well I vote that way because it represents your heart."

God: "Who said?"

Me: "You did."

God: "When?"

Me: "In the Bible! It's Your character isn't it?"

God: "Why did you assume that meant voting a particular way? Why do you vote the way you do?"

Me: "Out of principle, not self-interest."

God: "Whose principle?"

Me: "Yours."

God "Who said? Did you ever ask Me which way to vote?"

Light was starting to penetrate "I voted that way because I assumed that You would want me to without ever asking You. Okay, I get it. I have always voted presumptively without asking You."

This series of conversations over a few weeks early in 2016 are what opened the door to the possibility - no, the certainty - that I had many more assumptions and presumptions about God, the Bible, theology and doctrine than I ever thought –

and they all were veils and filters that prevented me knowing the true nature of God and His heart.

I started to discover that it is impossible to see God as He truly is when our minds are confused with our own distorted ideas about Him. Every time a mental stronghold is demolished, it makes way for a resurrection of fresh revelation. I did not find this an easy process as there was (and probably still is) a lot of humble pie to eat along the way.

Cognitive dissonance

I had a number of encounters with the Father in which He asked me to walk with Him. Those walks created cognitive dissonance within me. Cognitive dissonance is the mental stress (discomfort) experienced by a person who simultaneously holds two or more contradictory beliefs, ideas or values, when performing an action that contradicts those beliefs, ideas and values; or when confronted with new information that contradicts them. The encounters I had, walking with God, actually challenged what I believed about Him; what I thought I knew about God was called into question by my own experiences with Him.

On my first walk the Father led me to a familiar place deep in the garden of my own heart. This was the secret place of intimacy where it all began with the tree, swing and little bench. There, hanging in the branches of the tree, was an amazingly beautiful tapestry depicting my most intimate personal encounters with God. As I looked intently at the scenes woven into the fabric fond memories flooded back to my recollection. I noticed a small thread at the heart of the tapestry and I thought "I wonder if this will take me deeper if I follow it?" I reached out to lay hold of the thread and the whole tapestry unravelled before me leaving a pile of yarn on the grass. There was God laughing as I stood there perplexed.

He said, "You have framed all your experiences into that beautiful image! But... what is an image of me?"

"An idol."

"Exactly. You are leaning to your own understanding of Me, created from your encounters."

I felt deflated but God smiled and said "You don't need an understanding when you have a relationship of trust."

Trust in the Lord with all your heart and do not lean [or rely] on your own understanding. In all your ways acknowledge Him, and He will make your paths straight. Do not be wise in your own eyes... (Proverbs 3:5-7).

The Father took me on many more walks and opened up many encounters that I now see were designed to produce the cognitive dissonance which would bring deconstruction to my mind.

James Torrance puts it this way[4], "More important than our experience of Christ is the Christ of our experience." In your highest modes of enjoying Him, He is still more real than the experience itself. Language is insufficient to communicate His incommunicable nature. It must be experienced by encounters.

Andre Rabe says[5], "Jesus comes to make you an atheist to the god of your own making. He comes to bring an end to your way of subjecting God to your own understanding". I have concluded that I actually agree with Richard Dawkins and other well-known atheists in that I do not believe in that 'religious GOD' either.

It was only when I got to the place where my ideas and my faith were completely devastated that I could meet the God who transcends all our ideas about Him.

This is why so many Church Fathers and mystics have said something similar to this:

"To experience God is to experience the complete and utter failure of your own intellect" - Andre Rabe again.

As John Crowder points out[6], Jesus Himself was a deconstructionist. He was constantly challenging the prevailing religious paradigms of His day. He often said "You have heard it said (the rabbinical tradition)... but I say to you..." He completely challenged their thinking, turning religion on its head and unveiling the truth that everything is about love, not the do-it-yourself path of following dead works, duty and obligation.

I began to discover that God will not be confined to our limited, static perceptions of Him. We cannot keep an infinite God in a box constructed within the finite capacities of our understanding. All that will do is limit ourselves. God does not dwell in manmade temples, theological constructs or ideologies; He dwells in our spirits and in our hearts. We need to encounter Him so that we can have a transformation, a revolutionary change of mind. We need the veils of our understanding stripped away. This can only happen through our relationship with the living Word of Truth, the ultimate source of revelation who searches the deep things of God and makes them known to us.

Do not allow your current understanding to keep you in bondage to the imitations of your past experience. Insanity is to keep doing the same things expecting different results; it is to live trapped in our own limitations. Everything we receive must come through personal encounters with God. Those encounters will never contradict the record of God's nature and character revealed in the Bible but may not be directly found in it. They will definitely challenge religious belief systems which limit what the Bible actually says, by reducing it to a set of rules or doctrines.

Mistranslation

During this process of deconstruction, I have found that our English translations of the scriptures are not always the best guide. I have discovered that many words in the original languages are either left out, changed or mistranslated in our English versions. For example, 'the' is often left out before 'sin' or 'faith' when the definitive article should have been used. Or it is replaced with 'your', so that instead of 'the faith' it becomes 'your faith', which shifts the focus from what God gifts us to what we have to generate. Another example is the word 'of' being translated 'in' when used concerning faith: in Galatians 2:20 we live by faith of the Son of God and not (as most translations have it) by faith 'in' the Son of God.

The word 'repentance' is another example of an original Greek word being rendered into English in a way which completely changes the focus of its meaning. The Greek word is 'metanoia', which comes from 'meta', meaning together with, and 'nous', mind; thus, together with God's mind. This word suggests a radical mind-shift; it is to realise God's thoughts towards us, to think like God thinks about us. For this to happen we need to know how God thinks and that can be a major problem if we don't engage Him face to face. If we have a distorted view of God and of how He thinks and acts, we will have a distorted view of ourselves.

The word *metanoia* has been hijacked by religion and twisted. *Metanoia* is a change of mind, not being sorry for being caught. The English word 'repentance' is a religiously contrived word associated with 'penance'. 'Re-penance', with its blatant implication that payback is required for what we have done, is not what the Greek means at all!

We do not continually have to do penance for our past because Jesus dealt with that on the cross and made us righteous once and for all. We do need a *metanoia*, a radical shift of thinking, to enable a relationship with God in which we engage the Truth to reveal God's true reality and as a consequence our own true identity in sonship.

Or do you think lightly of the riches of His kindness and tolerance and patience, not knowing that the kindness of God leads you to repentance [metanoia]*?* (Romans 2:4 NASB).

Do not underestimate God's kindness. The wealth of his benevolence and his resolute refusal to let go of us is because he continues to hear the echo of his likeness in us! Thus his patient passion is to shepherd everyone into a radical mind shift. God believes in us way more than we believe in ourselves (Romans 2:4 MIR).

Religion has created a distorted view of God and therefore we often think of ourselves as slaves and not sons. This mistaken view can create a works mentality which causes us to try to appease or please GOD by our own actions or behaviour. It is a view of God that has come from the DIY tree path, the path of the tree of the knowledge of good and evil. If we follow that path we will be afraid of God and hide from Him while we try to make amends.

This leads to sin, another word which has been misused by religion to keep us in line through guilt, shame and condemnation. Our own DIY efforts can never bring righteousness. It is not something we can earn: we are already righteous because He made us righteous.

Concluding then that our righteousness has absolutely nothing to do with our ability to keep moral laws but that it is the immediate result of what Jesus accomplished on mankind's behalf, gives context to God's faith and finds expression in unhindered, face to face friendship with God! Jesus Christ is the head of this union! Jesus is God's grace embrace of the entire human race. So here we are, standing tall in the joyful bliss of our redeemed innocence! We are God's dream come true! This was God's idea all along! (Romans 5:1-2 MIR).

Sin is not our bad behaviours. Most uses of the word 'sin' or even 'sins' are preceded by the definite article, 'the sin', referring to the sin of Adam which was to follow his own path and do his own thing.

The corresponding Greek word *hamartia* does not mean 'missing the mark' either, as we are often told by a religion which tries to encourage us to hit the mark by self-effort. Sin is the loss of our image as sons and our attempts to restore that image by DIY methods. Sin is doing or being anything not aligned to our image and identity as sons.

My darling little children, the reason I write these things to you is so that you will not believe a lie about yourselves! If anyone does believe a distorted image to be their reality, we have Jesus Christ who defines our likeness face to face with the Father! He is our parakletos, the one who endorses our true identity, being both the source and the reflection of the Father's image in us! (The root of sin is to believe a lie about yourself. The word 'sin' is the word 'hamartia', from 'ha' = not, or negation, and martia from meros = a part of or share of, portion or form; thus to be without your allotted portion or without form, pointing to a disorientated, distorted, bankrupt identity; Sin is to live out of context with the blueprint of one's design; to behave out of tune with God's original harmony.) (1 John 2:1 MIR).

The English word 'hell', from Germanic and Norse roots, is used 56 times in the KJV and not even once in literal versions like Young's Literal Translation. There are 4 words translated 'hell': 'Sheol', 'Hades', 'Tartarus' and 'Gehenna', and none of them mean a place of eternal conscious torment.

The words 'eternal', 'everlasting', 'forever and ever' (which do not occur at all, relating to eternal conscious torment) are mistranslations of the Greek word *'ainios'* which actually means age-enduring, not a time without end.

Plumb line

So as God walked with me through encounters, I found I could not rely on my understanding of the Bible in English to give me a reference point in the midst of so much cognitive dissonance. I asked the Father one day "What do I use as my plumb line in the midst of so many subjective experiences?"

The Father said "Son, you can use agape love as your point of reference. If it is not love, it is not Me and if it is love, it is Me."

This is when I began to discover just how many assumptions and presumptions I was living according to. They related to God Himself and to so many doctrines and theological

187

positions that I had always thought true because that was what I had been taught, or that I had worked out from my own understanding.

All through this deconstruction process I have held to that agape love plumb line even when in pain. When God was challenging my understanding of controversial issues like 'hell', it felt like my head was going to explode. The stress on my brain felt like I had a restrictive steel band around my head. My mind felt more like it was being deconstructed rather than renewed but the end results were well worth the stress and pain I felt during the process.

And do not be conformed to this world, but be transformed by the renewing of your mind (Romans 12:2).

These two processes of non-conformation and transformation must run in parallel if our minds are to be renewed. We need to let go of the old DIY ways to embrace the new reality of our sonship with a new mind.

Live consistent with who you really are, inspired by the loving kindness of God... Do not allow current religious tradition to mold you into its pattern of reasoning. Like an inspired artist, give attention to the detail of God's desire to find expression in you. Become acquainted with perfection. To accommodate yourself to the delight and good pleasure of him will transform your thoughts afresh from within (Romans 12:1-2 MIR).

Renewing our minds will enable us to know God and therefore know our true selves and live in a new level of reality. We have not seen nor do we know anything yet.

God spoke to me during this process and said "Allow your mind and your consciousness to be expanded beyond all that you presently know and have experienced. Experience the reality of all that is, all that will be and most importantly all that can be within My heart. Son, let your monochrome existence become filled with my multi-coloured, multifaceted reality."

The walks I had with the Father were integral to the processes of deconstruction of my mind, allowing my mind to be remapped from the perspective of my eternal spirit's consciousness.

'Cardiognosis' is the knowledge of the heart. It is possible to know truth by impartation through encounters which are not cognitive but heart to heart or mind to mind. The mind of Christ is not a physical mind but a spiritual mind. To have the mind of Christ is to have a new consciousness and a new reality.

The mind of Christ

My encounters with God created cognitive dissonance within me but they also expanded my reality in relation to God and to myself. I had a choice, to fight and hold onto what I had thought to be true or to allow the Truth – Jesus – to renew my mind.

I had engaged God's heart many times with my spirit, outside the limitations of time and space, where my unrenewed linearly-processing mind could not function rationally. Then one day God said "Let me show you My mind". I expected flashing neurones and creativity energy of light-thoughts firing everywhere but that was far from what I actually experienced. I can't describe it visually as I don't have the words or the grid. It felt like being in the middle of a continuous harmonious conversation between Father, Son and Spirit. I heard faint echoes of my name spoken within those conversations as some of the vast sum of His thoughts about me (Psalm 139).

Then I heard the Father say "Let Me show you something". I got a brief glimpse of God's reality. I saw that God was connected to everyone that had ever lived, is living or will live, all at once: 108 billion and counting. He was connected to everyone in the 'now', knowing every thought, choice and every decision made every microsecond. I felt the depth of His loving desire to bring good out of every choice, to redeem even the most stupid decisions of every person.

And we know that God causes all things to work together for good to those who love God, to those who are called according to His purpose (Romans 8:28 NASB).

Meanwhile we know that the love of God causes everything to mutually contribute to our advantage. His Master Plan is announced in our original identity (Romans 8:28 MIR).

I felt totally overwhelmed and consumed by such amazing love and I was never able to see people in the same way again. The frustrations that I felt towards people seemed to fade away and my tolerance increased. That love was not limited to a select group of people who love God but is extended to everyone. The love of Father, Son and Spirit is expressed within the circle of conversation, communion, fellowship and oneness between God the one as three and the three as one.

God spoke to me from within that circle of love.

"Son, you can be one as We are one; your body, soul and spirit in oneness, unified and restored to godlikeness, to be the light of love to the world. Son, there is no ego or self within love.

190

Love that is God's is otherly, relational and conversational love and the essence of I AM is love. Love is light expressed as thoughts and desires concerning others.

"Son, sink deeper and deeper into Me. Let the conversation of love surround you and immerse you and fill you.

"Son, let the truth that love reveals define you, let it unveil your true image in Me. Son, you are, along with the whole of mankind, included in Me. So open the eyes of all your faculties to truly know who you are by reconnecting with who you have been." (He was referring to knowing our eternal spirit, not the reincarnation of our souls). "In Me, see your true image framed in love's conversation, revealed in love's true expression. Son, be from love's deepest well and let the spring become a fountain overflowing with love's energising power."

Another day Father said "Come, walk with Me". We began walking in His garden, a place of total rest. He said "I want to show you something" and I saw this amazing area within the Father's garden that was the most beautiful, living, vibrant place I had ever seen, felt, smelt or engaged with. The beauty of that area of cultivation was simply overwhelming, stimulating all my senses beyond my comprehension. Then the whole scene changed before my eyes into something very different in colour, form and fragrance but it again brought on equally amazing sensory overload; and then again it totally changed. I felt saturated emotionally but also totally confused. Then the Father said "Take a look through My eyes" and I caught just a glimpse of all the infinite possibilities all at once and I felt His pleasure and enjoyment. I now understood why God has created and crafted each person uniquely and the great love and affection He has for all of His creation. It was like a mind expanding trip that was to prepare me for what was to come.

The thought of having the mind of Christ (1 Corinthians 2:16) spun across my mind and for a fleeting second the possibility of nonlinear multi-dimensional living came into view.

Then God said "Son, walk with Me beyond beyond, to where you are destined to be". We walked through a doorway on Wisdom's heights onto the timeline of my life. I was in the past and present and saw the possibilities of what could be.

I saw multiple paths created by my mind and engaged by my choices. I saw where making no choice had and would take me; I saw where making wrong choices had and would take me. My first reaction was that I needed to know the right path to choose. Feelings of loss, regret and sadness started to overwhelm my emotions.

I felt the love of God and His pleasure for me wash all regret away and then it was as if my mind was being remapped. The consciousness of my spirit began to overshadow the consciousness of my soul and reconnect me to who I was. I saw the light, the energy and the atmosphere change. I saw myself as light, no longer a vestigial image of my present. The mists of long forgotten and unknown mysteries began to clear. I saw the new paths reconnecting my mind to areas of my consciousness that now stored the eternal memories of who I was.

As my consciousness entertained this new vista of eternal recollection, I saw the truth, the reality that once was, beginning to come into view. I saw myself within the mind of God as a son. I am as I have always been known as a desire in

God's heart and a conversation within His mind. I have a memory of the *Ya Sod* of God where I agreed my destiny scroll and where my angels were assigned.

Then the Father said again "Come and walk with me". We began to walk in a place which was dimly lit and it took time for my eyes to adjust. I had never been anywhere with the Father that was anything but brilliantly lit. There were light pathways crossing and connecting but it was as if the power was turned down and I was trying to get my bearings within a bowl of spaghetti.

"Son, you cannot see in this darkness because you are trying to look with the wrong eyes. Don't try to figure it out, just rest; be enveloped by the mystery of love hidden for you to discover here."

I asked "Where are we?"

"We are walking in your mind", the Father replied. Now I understood why it was so dimly lit! We continued to walk along paths of light until we came to a gulf that we could not cross. There were doors beyond the gulf which I somehow knew were only closed and not locked.

The Father said "Do you want me to bridge this gulf for you this once?" I did not hesitate and replied "Yes" I then saw a path extend to bridge the gulf. In that moment my mind was expanded and I sensed the possibility of new pathways developing in my mind. I was excited by the possibility of opening those doors to discover new dimensions or new realities. I felt and sensed the potential possibilities of the eternal reality of who I was always intended to be as a son. The capacities that have been locked and hidden could now begin to reconnect.

We walked across the light bridge and I looked for the Father to open the door. He looked at me and I knew I had to open it, so I reached out with my mind in my mind and the door opened – bizarre, but true.

I just gazed with amazement at the 'now'; beyond time and space I could see all the possible creative choices I could make at that one moment. My first reaction was "Which one do I choose?" That, I now realise, was a fear-based response founded in a wrong view of the nature of God. Because I was standing with the Father as a son, heart to heart, I immediately felt that fear just melt away.

I saw creative possibilities springing from my mind that were all good and all led to positive outcomes. I realised that all the possible creative choices were good and acceptable. My desire was focused and aligned to the heart of God but creatively I felt free as a son. I yielded and surrendered all that can be to become an expression of who I am in Him. I can make choices as a son to seek first God's kingdom and righteousness so that my creative choices will always be an expression of His ever-increasing government and peace.

These thoughts were rolling around my mind while I was standing in the depths of my mind. I started to focus and expand the eyes of my consciousness beyond the boundaries and limitations of my consciousness that have been disconnected from true reality. I saw that I could choose a possibility – that I could "pop the qwiff" in quantum language – and collapse the mystery and possibility into a reality.

Changing my reality

I came out of this encounter in which I had totally lost track of time, looked at my watch and saw that it was 7.45am. I was due in the office to see my friend Jeremy at 8am. My mind immediately saw the possibilities and I focused on the reality that I would keep that appointment without being late. I chose that reality and I felt totally at peace.

So I went upstairs and got showered, dressed and ready. When I came down I looked at the kitchen clock and it was 7.55am but my watch was still showing 7.45am. My watch is a Citizen Eco-Drive which never stops but now it was frozen in that moment. I decided to test this reality and went into the garden to water the greenhouse plants and feed the fish in the pond. When I came back in, my watch was still showing 7.45am but the kitchen clock now showed 8.10am. I was just about to leave when Deb, my wife, reminded me that she was having the car that day. It takes 2 to 3 minutes to get to the office by car but 10-15 minutes if you're walking. I said goodbye and started to walk. My watch stayed frozen at 7.45am until I got to about halfway, then time started to move again. I got to the office at 7.55am.

I have practised this ability to use my consciousness to create reality many times in different ways since then.

I have many testimonies with planes. One example was when I was flying from the UK to New Zealand, with a 1-hour stop in Hong Kong. We took off an hour late so I chose the reality where I arrived in time to catch my connecting flight. I was at rest and peaceful when an hour into the flight the co-pilot apologised about the delay and said that they had hoped to make up time but there was a strong headwind so we would land an hour late. I did not let the facts affect my peace. The thought came into my mind "I know an order of angels called Winds of Change" so I saw the reality where Winds of Change changed the wind direction. Within 30 minutes the co-pilot made another announcement: there had been a remarkable change in the wind direction and we now had a strong tail wind. In fact we arrived early and I caught my connecting flight with time to spare.

While in Auckland, New Zealand, I was speaking at a meeting about engaging the angelic realm. The meeting overran and by the time we left the building there was a queue of vehicles at the gate. I went to see what the problem was and found out that the caretaker had padlocked it and gone home. Several people had tried to open it but it was definitely locked. The first car in line was occupied by 2 ladies who were not yet believers, and they jokingly suggested that perhaps I could get an angel to open it. Instantly I saw the reality of an open gate. I said to them "No need for angels, I will open the gate." I went up to it and opened the lock without a key.

I have many similar testimonies about using the power of my consciousness to choose a reality in line with my destiny.

No longer bound by linearity

But this was not the major transformation that took place. I had been living in the dual realms of heaven and earth since 2012 but the next time I focused my soul's consciousness to engage my spirit in the heavenly realms, I discovered that my spirit's consciousness was no longer bound by linearity. Until this point my spirit was still engaging God in a linear fashion. I would yield myself as a living sacrifice, engaging the fire of the altar, engage the 4 faces of God in the Holy of Holies at the arc of God's presence in the tabernacle, step into the 4 faces and access the ancient paths back into God's heart outside of time and space. I would go to the courts or to Wisdom's Heights and eventually rule seated on the throne from my mountain.

Now I was able to be in all those places and more multi-dimensionally, free from linearity. I am not yet aware cognitively of everything at once but can shift the focus of my mind to engage each place as I am led to. Previously it was like a stream was flowing from wherever I was in the heavenlies, through my life as a gateway of heaven into the earth; but now there was an increase, like multiple streams flowing together into a river. Both my capacity and the flow of revelation and insight were multiplied greatly. As a result I was able to spend more time relationally engaging the Father, going deeper into the depths of God.

On yet another occasion the Father again said, "Son, walk with Me". We began to walk and this time I recognised that we were walking within the recesses of my mind, but on this occasion the focus was on how my consciousness was framed. The Father said "Son, look at the dysfunction of the broken paths. Look at the mind-sets that are like obstructions blocking the pathways. Son, look at the rigid networks conforming and framing the pathways within your mind."

Then I saw a different image: I could see a new potential, a mind with the fluidity and beauty of the pathways that can be formed by a renewed mind functioning as the mind of Christ. I saw the contrast between the simplicity of organic relational truth that was 'now', and the construction built up from the interpretations of truth and reality that come from religion and culture.

Pillars of my mind

The Father said "Son, let Me renew your mind to a new level. Open up your mind to Me. Let the truth remove the cages constructed by following the pathways of the knowledge of good and evil". I looked up and saw a framework, a construction like a grid, a series of connecting cross-members fixed to 9 pillars which were holding it up. The Father then started to shine a spotlight onto the pillars.

"Son, these are the pillars upon which your paradigms are built." He focused the light of truth on the first pillar of evangelicalism and then the pillar of Sola Scriptura. The light focused on the pillars of Greek and then Hebrew thought and exposed them as constructs of man. Then one by one the light focused on Augustinianism, Protestantism, Scientific Rationalism, Cultural Relativism and Humanism. I had to google some of those terms afterwards even to understand what they meant. These were the pillars that held up the framework of my belief systems, mind-sets and constructs of my consciousness.

I asked God about the 9 pillars and their origins. He gave me revelation about 9 stones that covered the light-bearer's body that were to reflect out the revelation of God.

..."You had the seal of perfection, Full of wisdom and perfect in beauty. You were in Eden, the garden of God; Every precious stone was your covering... {9 stones] ...On the day that you were created They were prepared. You were the anointed cherub who covers, And I placed you there. You were on the holy mountain of God; You walked in the midst of the stones of fire. You were blameless in your ways From the day you were created Until unrighteousness was found in you." (Ezekiel 28:12b-15).

The covering cherub's role was to absorb and reflect the light released from the throne of God. As the light bearer and musician of heaven, he was responsible to release frequencies that would carry the image of God that revealed our sonship. He chose another path, and he led mankind down it too: the DIY tree path. The 9 stones became counterfeited and perverted as 9 pillars that frame our minds. Each pillar controls how our mind interprets the data we receive, filtering the light of God and distorting both God's image and ours, creating mind-sets established from beliefs that someone has taught us, revelation from old theological truth meant for a previous day, the resting place of words that frame our belief systems. But there is a new revelation of truth to discover for our day.

God asked me if I wanted Him to deconstruct my mind. I said "Yes, Lord, deconstruct the frameworks of my mind, strip away the presumptions and the assumptions of my thinking. I want to think like a son".

Father said "Son, I can continue dismantling this from the outside in or I can remove the foundations of the dogma, the pillars and supports of the constructs so that they collapse. This may be traumatic and disorientating for a short while but it will be the most effective and quickest way to free your mind and consciousness from its constraints and restrictions".

I responded, "Father, please remove the pillars of my beliefs and restore the true foundations formed from eternal truth". Then I thought I might lose my mind so I quickly added "Please do it one at a time!"

As the pillars were ripped from my mind the constructs became increasingly unstable. It felt like my mind was wobbling, as if I was having a mind-quake. The truth began to challenge my beliefs and my mind started to become free from its restrictions. Then I started to see things I could not see before: the limitations were being removed and the realities were being expanded.

The Father continued to explode my mind. "Son, you are created and crafted with the creative nature of I AM as a son of God. Your true potential is limitless but is being controlled by the boundaries that exist within your consciousness.

"Son, rest in the deconstruction at the end of the 7th day to embrace the new beginnings of the 8th day reality. Son, I am the master of all reality: everything is contained within Me. I AM, therefore everything is contained within the infinite potential possibilities of My mind. You have access to My mind so that your mind can be conformed and freed from its limitations."

Thus says the Lord, "Stand by the ways and see and ask for the ancient paths, Where the good way is, and walk in it; And you will find rest for your souls..."(Jeremiah 6:16).

What reality are you living?

From whose perspective are you viewing reality? – yours or God's?

Does it feel like a dream or a nightmare?

Can you change your reality?

We all see the world through a lens that filters life's experiences and gives us a conformational-biased view, tending to perpetuate the status quo. All reality or truth, if not seen through the perspective of The Truth, Jesus himself, will eventually become a nightmare. Our minds are constructed and supported by the pillars of beliefs and value systems that have been built through the experiences of our lives. Those pillars form our worldviews and frame how we interpret the world around us; they are our conscious reality. The pillars in our minds may be revealed as lies or false representations of reality when viewed in comparison with The Truth, Jesus, who is the only true reality. Many of my constructs were built around religious theology or doctrine (Evangelicalism, Sola Scriptura, Greek thought, Hebrew thought, Augustinianism, Protestantism) whilst others were from the education system and from the DIY tree path of self (Scientific Rationalism, Cultural Relativism, Humanism).

"When your mind is stretched by a big idea it will never return to its original shape" (Thomas Carlyle).

Once the first pillar was removed (evangelicalism), the theological belief systems began to crumble and collapse like a domino rally. Doctrines and theological positions not reflecting God's love began to be exposed as lies – exposed by the light of truth.

I began to see things I never saw before, connected with people who were invisible to me before. Long-held beliefs were challenged by the experiences of God's love I had through encountering and engaging with Him. My whole relationship with God began to change as my filters were removed and I started to see everything through the lens of love.

Tree of Life

I asked the Father "What is going to replace those constructs?"

"Son, let Me form the pathways of the tree of life within the construct of your mind. Let Me reform and connect the ancient paths within your brain so that your consciousness will become unrestricted and your creative potential will not be limited. I must plant new roots within your mind that will be able to flow from the eternal source, let them be entwined as the pathways to truth. As the living Word, My relationship with you can now be the first pathway that will become a trunk that supports life."

I felt this root system of truth begin to form deep in my mind.

I had had an encounter with Wisdom a few years before in which she gave me a seal and a staff and took me through a door on her heights. We walked through a fiery tunnel until we stood before a large door guarded by a creature that I can only describe as looking like the Balrog from *The Lord of the Rings*. Staying with the LOTR theme, the thought of Gandalf came to me and I slammed my staff with the seal on top into the ground and demanded to pass. The creature stepped aside and the door opened. This place felt oddly familiar; not in a visual sense but because of the feelings of constriction, oppression and claustrophobia it produced.

This was Satan's trophy room, and the atmosphere felt heavy with sadness. I could see the destinies of not yet believers on display as diamonds and there were mantles and scrolls robbed from past and present. The area I was most drawn to was called heritage, and here I was able to connect with my four family lines. I felt angry that I had not received much of a Christian heritage, apart from only 2 generations on my maternal grandfather's side and the generation of my great grandmother, on my paternal grandmother's side. It seemed like there were multitudes in my ancestry who had never found their destiny and that I had lost my inheritance spiritually. I sensed from

Wisdom that all of that heritage could be restored in my generation. I was excited about the prospect of all that had been robbed being restored but I had no clue how or when that might happen.

This place also reminded me of a vision I had about 10 years ago where I engaged an angel and we went into a lift that I assumed was going to heaven. Then it started to descend instead, which felt very odd. As the lift stopped and the door opened I walked out into a huge vast plain with a rainbow in the distance. I walked excitedly towards the rainbow, eventually realising that it appeared to form an arch that was like a wall with many brightly coloured attractive doors. With great anticipation, I opened a door and walked in. Immediately I felt trapped in a black enclosed space so claustrophobic that I backed out in panic, shocked by the feelings of restriction and oppression. I backed off to look more closely at the arch and noticed that colours of the rainbow were inverted and that each of the doors had numerous little hooks covering them hidden by the bright colours. I realised that I had been deceived by external appearances.

I went back to the lift where the angel was waiting and this time we ascended, going up beyond our entrance point. When the door opened, I stepped out into a kind of anteroom with one small ordinary-looking door which had a keyhole but no handle. Learning from my previous mistake, I looked closely and observed that the lock was shaped like a heart. In the vision I felt that only giving my heart would open the door so I reached into my body, took my heart and put it into the lock. The door immediately opened and I could see a vast bright colourful expanse. I did not feel free to enter but I sensed love, joy and peace filling the atmosphere. There was a total freedom from the restrictions characteristic of the previous place.

New versus Old

During the process of deconstruction I started to examine some of the things I believed from the perspective of new versus old. Many people who are exploring beyond the veil talk of the new and the old. I began to meditate on these thoughts to expose my mind to the critical eye of God, so that I would be able to see where I was still thinking from an old earthly perspective, rather than from the perspective of heaven. I decided it would be good to share just a few sessions of teaching on the subject but in the end it turned into a 47-session series! The theological dominoes just fell one after the other as my eyes were opened to the truth. Having a passion and a mandate for a harvest of souls, I began looking at evangelism. This challenged my whole view of what the good news is and how we present it. My encounters with God as love challenged so many assumed theological and doctrinal positions which were put under the microscope with the lens of love. Fear-based 'turn or burn' evangelism did not line up with a God who, as perfect love, casts out all fear.

I discovered an apparent dichotomy between the two-faced God who is angry and needs to be appeased by blood sacrifices in the Old Testament and the loving Father revealed by Jesus in the New. The angry, distant deity (GOD) who punishes people, the cosmic child abuser who killed His own Son on the cross, stands in sharp contrast to the loving Father who so loves the world.

The doctrines that support the orthodox understanding of GOD just could not be maintained looking through the lens of love. False assumptions began to unravel, including the nature of judgment and justice, penal substitutionary atonement (PSA), eternal conscious torment (ECT), eternal damnation in hell, and death as the end of choice, to mention just a few.

And as I previously shared, when I tried to engage the Bible to help make sense of it all, I found I really could not trust the way it had been translated into English. The issues of salvation, inclusion, universalism, death and hell began to be unravelled. My head felt like it was exploding with mind-quakes, rocking and shaking the very core foundations of my beliefs. The more I engaged God and discovered the very essence and nature of His love, the more I found that what I had been taught as the foundations of the Christian faith were not the beliefs of the first disciples or the early Church Fathers. I traced the 'orthodoxy' of modern evangelicalism through the protestant reformation and theologians like Calvin, back to views which were an invention of Tertullian and Augustine, propagated and enshrined in our interpretation of the scriptures by Jerome's translation of the Bible into Latin, the Vulgate.

Evangelicalism has a 500 year old history of making Christianity mainly a rational and theological understanding about God, rather than an actual ongoing personal, experiential encounter with Him. A living encounter with the living God beats a theology about Him any day! (Mark Virkler).

Satan's trophy room revisited

Shaken by my encounters and the discoveries they unveiled, I asked the Father for experiential confirmation through the living Word of God, Jesus, the Way, the Truth and the Life. Jesus took me to Wisdom's heights and through the familiar door through the fire to Satan's trophy room. We engaged the area of heritage as I had seen before and I felt drawn to my paternal grandfather's family line. Jesus looked at me and asked if I wanted to engage with it. I did not understand what He meant but felt compelled to say "Yes". He gave me a silver trumpet and pointed towards a door that I had not seen there before.

I asked, "Where did that door come from?" Smiling, Jesus said, "It has always been here but your mind would not allow you to see it".

The door opened and we walked into a place I could only describe as fire but as I discovered myself, when engaging the fires of the judgment seat or the altar, this was also a manifestation of God who is a consuming fire. Fire is an expression of God's love, not punishment, and what I observed was multitudes of people standing consumed by fire, in anguish or torment of soul facing the reality of their life's choices. There were no demons or devils with pitchforks – those ideas are more aligned with Dante's *Inferno* and Hieronymus Bosch's paintings than the reality of what I was seeing – and God was certainly not punishing, torturing or tormenting anyone either.

I began to think about my experiences in the fire of God's presence, engaging the Seraphim, and what it might be like without knowing the love of God as I do. I was overawed but inspired. I had renewed great passion to preach the gospel so that no one would have to go there. I looked at Jesus and He was saying nothing. So rather tongue-tied and feebly I began to preach the good news. When I finished, Jesus turned to walk out and I thought "I am not staying here on my own". Noticing the silver trumpet in my hand I thought I had better blow it, so on my way to the door I did so. We walked what seemed like a long way through the fiery tunnel and back through the door which now had the appearance of a fiery sword. We turned towards the door and I saw that some people had followed us through the fire and as they approached the door they kneeled and I heard them confess Jesus as Lord and walk through the door, entering through the gate into Zion.

I turned to look at Jesus and said "What have you done to me now? I am ruined! What am I supposed to say to people?" Jesus smiled again and said "Tell them that you are doing what I did, and that I have told everyone to do what I did and greater."

I then asked why more people did not respond, aside from my feeble preaching. Jesus replied that people have free will to choose and they can hold onto their self-righteousness but also that my authority to preach to my generational line is proportional to the amount of fire that has purified it. I decided to spend more time focused on the altar, as described in Isaiah 6, where the prophet saw that he had unclean lips and came from a generational line of people with unclean lips. The fiery coal from the altar purified him and dealt with the generational issues. Having engaged that altar since, I have been back to the fire many times now for each of my family lines with varying degrees of success – but tens of thousands have responded, accepting and confessing Jesus as Lord and joining the ranks of the cloud of witnesses.

On one specific occasion I was speaking in China in 2017 and, unusually for me, I woke up at 3am with a specific thought about the issue of divorce in my father's generational line. My father was divorced, as was my grandfather but I know nothing about previous generations so that is as far back as I can go. I immediately focused on engaging the fire of the altar. As I presented the issue I felt that all my generational lines were involved. I began to forgive and release them from the debt outstanding against them as I did felt an overwhelming sense of compassion and love for them. I was moved to engage immediately with the consuming fire of God's presence where I began to preach the good news of forgiveness from the guilt, shame and condemnation of divorce and infidelity. I blew the silver trumpet and noticed that a vast number followed me out, following the same pattern. Since beginning to share this publicly as others are now doing, I have had many emails and messages thanking me because others have had similar experiences but have been apprehensive to share them for fear of being branded a heretic. I am very happy to accept the accusation based on this adaptation of the acronym coined by Chuck Crisco, a fellow traveller:

Happy Enlightened Righteous Exploring Truth In Christ

I found that the view commonly held up as orthodoxy by the evangelical majority was not the orthodox position held by most of the early Church Fathers and by many throughout church history. As a result I have, of course, been accused of abandoning orthodoxy myself. In one online debate I asked if my accuser could point to even one scripture which categorically states that we lose the ability to choose Jesus after physical death. Of course they could not, as such a scripture does not exist. It would be strange indeed if death, which has been conquered and swallowed up in victory, had the power to change the character of God.

My point in writing about this is to highlight how, according to orthodoxy, God who (before people die) is rich in kindness, tolerance and patience towards everyone (according to Romans 2:4), in the hope that they will have a shift of thinking *(metanoia)* to agree with God about their salvation in Christ, then suddenly (after they die) apparently no longer has any of those attributes and instead torments and punishes people forever.

The loving Father of the whole of creation who has in fact reconciled the cosmos and therefore every single human being to Himself in Christ, not counting their sins against them (according to 2 Corinthians 5:18-19), is my Dad whom I have come to know and who is fathering me as His son. God who has reconciled everyone to Himself wants everyone to choose to accept His loving kindness and be reconciled to Him.

To clarify, I am not a Universalist who believes all religious roads lead to relationship with God as Father. That only comes through Jesus, the Way, the Truth and the Life. I am not even a Christian Universalist who believes that it is guaranteed that everyone will eventually accept Jesus as Lord, as that removes the element of personal choice. I do know that God as a loving Father will never, ever, give up on any of His children and that His love will never fail. So I am hopeful that everyone will one day accept Jesus – but it is not automatic and cannot be guaranteed.

Those critics who use arguments such as "In that case there is no point preaching the gospel" or "We might as well just keeping sinning if there is no hell as a consequence" have missed the point entirely. I would not want anyone in this age or the ages to come to miss out on their full inheritance as a son of God, so I am more passionate than ever about preaching the good news. There are very clear consequences to sin both in this age and within the fire of God's purifying love but to suggest that we need the law and fear to motivate us to be good shows a completely wrong understanding of the character and nature of God.

"I have sworn by Myself, The word has gone forth from My mouth in righteousness And will not turn back, That to Me every knee will bow, every tongue will swear allegiance" (Isaiah 45:23).

...so that at the name of Jesus every knee will bow, of those who are in heaven and on earth and under the earth, and that every tongue will confess that Jesus Christ is Lord, to the glory of God the Father (Philippians 2:10-11).

Now all these things are from God, who reconciled us to Himself through Christ and gave us the ministry of reconciliation, namely, that God was in Christ reconciling the world to Himself, not counting their trespasses against them, and He has committed to us the word of reconciliation (2 Corinthians 5:18-19).

There is plenty of biblical warrant for Jesus going to Hades and preaching to those in prison where He led captivity captive. It is not within the scope of this book to defend these experiences; I have done so already in numerous teaching sessions in which I go into this in more depth. There are also some other excellent resources available. I am not writing to try to get you to change your doctrine to. I am just sharing my journey and experiences with the hope that you will be open to seek the truth for yourself with an open mind.

Why is deconstruction and renewal necessary?

"...and that He may send Jesus, the Christ appointed for you, whom heaven must receive until the period of restoration of all things about which God spoke by the mouth of His holy prophets from ancient time" (Acts 3:20-21).

We are tasked with the restoration of all things, but that is impossible if we still have limitations. We are not going to fix the problem with the same DIY methods that created it. We are not going to build embassies of heaven in the way they built at Babel, to make a name for themselves. We will have the ability to construct organically using quantum reality.

The Spirit Himself testifies with our spirit that we are children of God, and if children, heirs also, heirs of God and fellow heirs with Christ... For the anxious longing of the creation waits eagerly for the revealing of the sons of God... that the creation itself also will be set free from its slavery to corruption into the freedom of the glory of the children of God (Romans 8:16-17, 19, 21 NASB).

His Spirit resonates within our spirit to confirm the fact that we originate in God. Because we are his offspring, we qualify to be heirs; God himself is our portion, we co-inherit with Christ. Since we were represented and included in his suffering we equally participate in the glory of his resurrection... Our lives now represent the one event every creature anticipates with held breath, standing on tip-toe as it were to witness the unveiling of the sons of God. Can you hear the drum-roll?... All creation knows that the glorious liberty of the sons of God sets the stage for their own release from decay. We sense the universal agony and pain recorded in history until this very moment. We ourselves feel the grief echo of their groaning within us while we are ready to embrace the original blueprint also of our physical

211

stature to the full consequence of sonship. What we already now participate in as first fruits of the Spirit will bloom into a full gathering of the harvest. (God loves the whole cosmos but it is waiting for us to mature as sons. Sons who know the truth and full reality about their Father and themselves) (Romans 8:16-17, 19, 21-23 MIR).

We need to see God as He truly is and see ourselves as created in His image. The illusions and delusions must be exposed so that we can be unplugged from this false reality. Jesus the Truth, the last Adam, desires to remove the limits placed on us by the first Adam; desires to restore us and conform us to our original eternal blueprint, able to engage bandwidths of energy, abilities regained which were lost at the fall, the flood and Babel.

Only the Truth that I am conscious of and know by experience will set me free from being tethered to the earth (the physical realm) and being under its rule and bondage. The Truth desires to release us into the glorious freedom of our sonship as co-heirs of His kingdom. Our conscious thought has quantum power. The universe responds to the focus of our consciousness. We have the mind of Christ, and therefore the capacity for the 'greater works' He promises (see John 14:12). It is time to embrace the potential possibilities of who we are because of who He is.

Creating reality

One of the core principles of Quantum Physics is the idea that reality (the photons which produce the light-illusion we all occupy) exists in infinite possible states (the 'many worlds' scenario) until we observe it and thus collapse all potential versions of reality into the one single option we've chosen to live inside.

Consider this. One evening you are sitting on your sofa and you are suddenly struck with the desire to do something different. You are suddenly faced with the decision between infinite permutations of reality; you could do an infinite number of different things.

You could go to the bathroom. You could switch on the light; you could walk outside; you could go to the kitchen, you could turn on the TV or your computer or phone. You could go to the off licence (liquor store) or you could go to your drug dealer.

As you weigh things up, what you start to focus on becomes more likely to occur. Past rewards and memories can drive you towards your choice and reality. You can immerse your consciousness into any reality you want. But you must decide which action you will take, you must make a choice, about which reality you want to 'observe' at the cost of becoming 'blind' to all other options. This is where compulsive behaviours driven by our past choices can overwhelm us.

As soon as you select a reality and move towards that observed choice, suddenly the photons around you blur and shift as you pull yourself deeper into that reality; the options you did not select, however, now fade out of conscious thought, out of observation, and thus begin to experience a decay of quantum likelihood as you continually move away from them in pursuit of your selected reality.

But that option which you did select – well, its photons are now becoming more vivid, turning from abstract imaginary choice into tangible forms you can interact with (whether it's the light switch, the TV, bathroom, drink, drug or image, etc.). This is a simple example of how this concept works, how your internal consciousness, those synapses and chemicals manipulated by your thoughts, can alter the physical photons that surround you.

So whose reality do you want to create and from which source do you draw on to make your choice? God or DIY?

If you are choosing from your past, you may be:

- Hiding your passion and creativity because you're afraid you may not be good enough (such as not doing art because someone told you that you were rubbish at it).
- Not pursuing a passion because someone told you it was a silly pastime that would never make you money.
- Agreeing to plans you don't really want to be a part of, just to fit in.
- Staying in a job or relationship that doesn't fulfil you because you need the money.
- Not taking the time to look for other jobs for fear of switching to something new.
- Not going after jobs that would make you happier but may not be as financially stable.
- Pursuing relationships that you know aren't healthy because you don't want to be alone.

Our present reality is the product of being controlled by the programming of our past experiences and knowledge. Our future reality will continue to be a self-perpetuating fulfilment of our past, unless we see from a new heavenly reality perspective.

If you do decide to escape your own source, you have the power to envision a future reality that doesn't currently exist, so rather than simply choosing the option you wish to engage with from an existing menu, you can instead create new photon-forms which never existed before and inject them into reality.

We have this incredible ability called imagination: the ability to mentally envision a thing or a concept and then summon it into reality. We all have that ability but do we use it? All the things you see today: buildings, cars, planes, tables, chairs, computers, even the clothes on your body, these are all physical items we can now choose to interact with even though they originally only existed as thought forms inside someone's mind. They were all once inert pieces of quantum possibility floating in the abstract realm of human imagination, until someone came along and had the means to choose to pursue their creation.

What reality are we creating for our lives?

By faith we understand that the worlds were prepared by the word of God, so that what is seen was not made out of things which are visible (Hebrews 11:3).

...even God, who gives life to the dead and calls into being that which does not exist (Romans 4:17 NASB).

...and is calling the things that be not as being (Romans 4:17 YLT).

From whose perspective are you viewing yourself?

What reality are you creating from your observation?

Are you perpetuating a reality based on what you already know or have already experienced?

This quantum wave collapse - caused by observation - is called 'popping a qwiff'. You can see or observe a God qwiff (something God shows you that is not yet real in this dimension) and, by observing or popping that qwiff, cause that potential to become your reality.

"Information flowing from your future possibilities is waiting for you to see – to observe and call those things that are not as though they are. The quantum leap of knowing your purpose and assignment is waiting as a God qwiff for you to pop!" (David Van Koevering[8]).

God has dignified man by giving him free will to choose and create his own reality aligned to those choices. Those choices made independently of God have created the existing chaotic DIY state of the world. They are created without the reference point of love. When we are reconciled and restored in relationship with God Himself, our mind can be renewed. This opens up the potential possibilities that we are able to access in the eternal mind of God, so that our future reality can be realigned from an eternal godly perspective. If you continue to use the DIY methods such as drugs, alcohol, pornography, food, relationships, religious works or any other substitute then your addiction to DIY will keep you in bondage. Choose another future, see another reality; see your freedom and your God-given destiny.

Quantum observation, quantum entanglement, quantum tunnelling and quantum faith all become abilities empowered by our expanded consciousness conformed to the mind of Christ.

Freedom from addiction: can you see that reality?

Freedom from sickness, disease and pain: can you see that reality?

Freedom from rejection, fear, insecurity, poverty and every bondage and limitation: can you see those realities?

If we cannot see them as truth then they cannot manifest in our lives.

"You will know the truth and the truth will set you free! ... So if the Son [The Truth] *sets you free, you will be free indeed"* (John 8:32, 36 NIV).

We can be free from the chains of time and space and the dimensional restrictions of the matrix of our belief systems and mind-sets, free to fly untethered and unrestricted.

There can be many realities, but there is only One Truth. The Truth, once perceived, may not always be to our taste; it may not always be convenient or pleasant, as it means change. It will often require sacrifice and discipline but it will always bring us freedom. When we turn from the Truth and return to pseudo-realities, it is either because we fear the hardships and responsibilities that freedom brings, or because we lose sight of the higher purpose.

If we are not "unplugged", we will find the truth unpalatable and hard because of our DIY mind-sets. If we cannot perceive the eternal realm of which we are citizens, we will remain confined and tethered to this earthly, DIY version of reality: earthbound, restricted and living in a carefully constructed illusion which limits us to being 'mere mortals', unable to change anything or fulfil our destiny.

...in whose case the god of this world has blinded the minds of the unbelieving so that they might not see the light of the gospel of the glory of Christ, who is the image of God (2 Corinthians 4:4).

Are you blinded by the world's DIY system? Whose reality are you living in?

Much supernatural truth has been veiled and perverted by the New Age movement and is put 'off limits' to us by the religious spirits operating within the old order religious systems. We must recover that hijacked truth. All truth is from God because Jesus is the Truth but some things have been veiled in deception. The veil is the construct of deception which has robbed us of true reality, but when we come to know the Truth we can experience that true reality.

True reality is not what we have come to know through our earthly experiences; therefore we have been living in an illusion veiled as reality (some scientists believe that our universe behaves very much as if it is a holographic projection[7]). What is your reality? Is your reality shaped by what you have experienced and what you have seen? Can you trust what you see? Where are you looking for your reality? Is your truth relative or absolute?

Our consciousness is a series of electrical impulses in our synapses, passing along neural pathways, which our brain interprets as thoughts. We have learnt to interpret those signals. We can also use those signals. In fact the world of matter and energy responds to us when we learn to focus on those signals.

Everything depends on your perspective when you look at it. Your consciousness has the ability to affect energy and matter from a quantum perspective. Light is an energy wave that carries the potential to become a matter particle depending on the thought of the viewer. This Truth may be beyond what I can presently imagine or think. Renewing our minds is the expanding of our consciousness to know our true potential.

God has chosen the foolish things to confound the wise (1 Corinthians 1:27 MEV) so we would know that it is only through Jesus we can know the Truth. Our minds must be enlightened or illuminated by the light of Truth, the vast sum of God's thoughts about me (Psalm 139:17) which reveal that I am a son of God, created in His image, with a destiny to rule the universe with Him. That truth will unlock the true potential of our sonship, the creative image in which we are made.

For this reason it says, "Awake, sleeper, And arise from the dead, And Christ will shine on you" (Ephesians 5:14).

Waking up to knowing the Truth as a person will set us free to be whom God intended us to be. It will challenge our present perception of ourselves. We can know the truth from God's perspective and align ourselves with His thoughts about us. We can see ourselves free from addiction; we can see ourselves healed; we can see ourselves loved, accepted, affirmed, significant. We can see ourselves fulfilling our destiny.

Let's be creative sons of God not limited by our DIY pasts and so able to create a better future. All of creation has its eyes fixed on us looking for true sons to be revealed.

Will you be one of those sons?

Will you accept the call?

Will you embrace your destiny?

Will you accept His yoke and learn from Him, the Truth?

He is calling for the sons of God to arise.

Postscript: The Golden River

In November 2017, Rebecca Harris, one of our Ekklesia Bench of Three, had a prophetic revelation about God calling us to engage a golden river that was going to cascade out of heaven. We spent a few weeks preparing for this event by dealing with past disappointments, unfulfilled expectations and dreams. We set the date to engage with the river

for Sunday December 3rd 2017. I began to seek for more revelation about the purpose of the golden river invitation.

During a time of engaging the Father He shared the following:

"Sons, the golden river is a point of convergence where time and eternity meet to create a *kairos* moment of *kainos* golden opportunity.

"This is the convergence of 7 rivers of spirit baptisms: life, grace, mercy, love, joy, peace and fire. These have been released through the windows of heaven, cascading down like waterfalls to join here into one glorious heavenly flow.

"The 7 spirits of God are here to mandate, equip, authorise, prepare, reveal and empower you for your position as a son.

"The 7 colours of the redemptive gifts are flowing within the river to connect you to your redemptive destiny within the restoration of all things.

"It is an opportunity to connect to your eternal destiny and be part of a great shift. The river is flowing with grace and faith to restore your identity and equip you for new positions of kingdom governmental authority.

"Embrace the river and bathe in it. Be immersed and filled with a new and fresh momentum to propel you forward towards your destiny as sons of God.

"This convergence of time and eternity is designed to be a time of integration where the pain of lost identity is healed and wholeness is restored.

"This is your moment where time will be suspended for you to reconnect and restore past and present to remove all dichotomies and divergences to become whole.

"This river is flowing from my heart and is filled with My glory expressed as the vast sum of My thoughts about each of you revealing the pattern of My original intention.

"In this river you can see your glory, the essence of your true identity, your true image of eternal sonship.

"Embrace the flow so you can be transfigured in light and reconciled to eternity, so that all fragments and fractures within your soul's identity can be harmoniously restored to the light, frequency and fragrance of your eternal position within creation.

"Within the flow is the sound of many waters: My voice calling out your name, calling you to sonship, calling you to resonate with the frequency of My heart.

"Sons, hear the call of My voice and be transformed and conformed to the original image of your design, behold and become."

I was excited and - as I thought - prepared.

On December 2nd we held a regional event with Justin Paul Abraham called "Heaven Changing Earth" in Exeter, our nearest city. During the evening session Lindy Strong, a member of the regional Bench of Three, was facilitating some encounters. I entered into them enthusiastically until I was arrested by the Father with a pronouncement that He needed to do open heart surgery. I gingerly accepted the invitation and in this vision He opened my chest and proceeded to reveal that there were figuratively two blocked valves in my heart. He showed me that I have a greater capacity to receive into my heart than can flow out. I fully responded by giving Him permission to restore the valves to original condition. The valves were unblocked giving an increased capacity flow heaven into the earth.

I was now even more excited by the golden river invitation. Sunday morning arrived and while spending some intimate time with the Father I saw the room set up with flags according to the seven colours of the rainbow to represent the golden river. I arrived early and put out the flags so that we could physically engage in what God was going to do spiritually.

Engaging the golden river

I first engaged Wisdom and Knowledge in the spirit.

I stepped into the river at the violet end and immediately felt an increase as I engaged the Spirit of the Fear of the Lord. The motives of my heart started to come into the light of glory and my destiny as I began to reconnect to my eternal identity. I connected to the groan of creation with the emotions from 'what was', despair, despondency; then I began to be filled with a new hope and a stronger passion for restoration.

223

I felt an overwhelming sense of compassion for the restoration of my heritage for my family lines and I immediately went to the consuming fire of God's love. With great boldness I began to preach the good news about restoration and healing from fracturedness, brokenness, despair and deception. I shared about the power of the cross to heal, restore and make the soul whole. I pleaded with each of my family lines in turn to respond to the gospel and accept Jesus as Lord. I asked Jesus to come as the Prince of Peace and minister wholeness. I called to the fractured parts of those who were broken and fragmented to come together into the Prince of Peace Jesus. What happened next was a blur of activity as it seemed everyone was responding to the invitation of peace and wholeness.

I blew the silver trumpet and beckoned them to follow me. I felt hope fill the atmosphere and I walked out with multitudes following me through the fiery sword. I was overjoyed that virtually everyone responded. Then Jesus gave me a scroll with a new mandate for specific people groups, those who had been deceived by religion and the false hopes of the New Age in their search for spiritual truth.

As I stepped forward I found myself in the library of heaven but this time my soul's previously insatiable need to know was resting in trust in my Dad. I began to absorb book after book into my spirit as a constant stream of true knowledge flooded into me. I seemed to have an increased capacity to know and an increased capacity to love.

I stepped forward onto the blue flag and was given a greater glimpse into my role as a son in the 'what was' before time and that strengthened me to accept my present and future roles within the restoration of all things. I reconnected with my role as a light bearer and catalyst of reconciliation dimensionally. The desire to see restoration between factions dimensionally began to surge within me like I was feeling a new rhythm from the Father's heart and I started to pulse with energy and focus.

I stepped forward towards green and yellow and I was filled with a new sense of purpose that was stirred by a recollection of the intention of God's heart for peace. I felt love as thoughts of harmonious union flooding my mind and my emotions. I really started to feel the convergence of time and eternity with a kairos moment of clarity and singularity. The restored hope of the ages struck me as pulses of light and truth to inspire, stimulate and catalyse me to change. My tasks that had been hidden as mysteries by the Father's cloud came into view: I carry a sound frequency and fragrance that are designed to release the patterns and memory of what was and is and will be; I am to radiate the hope of recollection that will cause desire for the harmony of mystic union. The union of spirit, soul and body within the heart of the Father's intent, reconnecting with union of earth and heaven; that is the spark for reconciliation and restoration of all things within the seen and unseen realms and between dimensions and races divided.

The books of the library of heaven are filled both with history and possibility and I absorbed the restored truth and perspective.

I continued and felt wisdom imparted for future missions in the restoration process. The desire and passion for restoration had increased and the limitations and fears fell away as the possibilities became probabilities within my mind. I sensed that the knowledge of the ancients and the abilities of old are being restored.

This was a profoundly powerful experience, the most intense I have experienced this side of the veil.

In the days that followed the Father began to speak to me more directly and clearly open up the mysteries that had been but faint impressions.

"Son, prepare now for what is about to come and be ready. Stir my people to realise that they are My children so they will recognise their sonship and take their places in the government of heaven.

"Prepare for the shift that is coming by looking to Wisdom's pillars and engaging in the heavenly assemblies where the times and seasons are being set. Draw from My heart and come deeper into the depths of love. The secrets and hidden mysteries are yours to discover. Son, raise the expectancy by revealing the potential for possibilities that you have seen and the creative realities that you can choose from within the depths of love.

"Son, voice control is an illustration of what your minds are designed to accomplish by the power of your consciousness. When you know your identity, creation will respond to the power of your thoughts and words to be set free into the glorious essence of your sonship.

"Son, call and keep calling to creation to be restored to be free and to be made whole in true peace. Create expectancy within creation itself for freedom. Issue the answer to the groaning with a new sound of hope. Son, be the sound, carry the frequency; walk as a gateway of heaven's hope wherever you go in the seen and unseen realms.

"Son, call for the establishment of a new vista to see a new horizon from a whole new dimensional perspective. See new beginnings, new priorities, new opportunities, new adventures, new identities, new roles, new positions, new levels of experience, new dimensions. Behold, see, I am the God of the new because to Me everything is always new and always old but I always see from the optimistic perspective. Everything is being restored to be like new as it is from My viewpoint. 'I am that I am' is a statement of My being and My doing. I am is who I am. I live in the beginning and the end, the *alpha* and the *omega*, the *Aleph* and the *Tav;* therefore nothing is impossible, there is nothing that cannot be restored.

"Son, 'all things' means 'all things' but I choose to do everything relationally in love. So things are constantly and continually being renewed as My children discover the truth of their identity in the circle of My relationship, take their places and accept their responsibilities as sons of God.

"Son, you have glimpsed the reality which is My heart and My mind. You know how I am at work throughout time and space, continually in the 'now', working out the new to conform it to My loving intention. Restoration is not an event but a continuous and continual realignment of free will choices, framing them in love's opportunities. Son, love has won, love is winning and love will win because love never fails. It is totally consistent, completely trustworthy, reliable and faithful. Son, love has conquered, love is conquering and love will conquer and overcome all obstacles, hindrances, obstructions, distractions and divergences. I am love and what Paul expressed to the Romans was what he saw and experienced when I opened My heart to him. Who can be separated from the love of God? No one! This was not a limited statement from a limited atonement but an all-inclusive proclamation of love's overcoming power. Nothing can be separated from love (nor, by definition, from Me) because as love all live and move, exist and have their being in Me. Son, the power of love is supremely sovereign and can never fail as Paul again observed and expressed to the Corinthians. The power of love is unlimited, unrestricted, boundless, abundant, lavish, extreme, radical, effulgent, overflowing, indulgent, untameable, immovable, intransigent."

Finally here is my most recent encounter, on June 20th 2018.

"Son, let Me show you something. Come walk with Me. Here in the Mantles House [one of the twelve High Chancellors' houses] there are many new mantles being prepared for this generation so My children can become men and women after My own heart who will serve My purposes in this their generation and inspire the next generation to rise up and walk together. See the new roles and responsibilities that are being prepared to align with destiny and redemptive gift."

There was a great deal of activity going on in the Mantles House, with many angelic beings working on rows and rows of mantles of many different colours, sizes and materials.

"Son, will you try on this new mantle? You don't need to take off the old; this is in addition to your eternal mantle."

I was drawn to a red and orange mantle of a matt, non-reflective material. The angel fitted it over my shoulders and immediately the Spirit of Wisdom, the Spirit of Knowledge and the Spirit of the Lord, 3 of the 7 spirits of God, came around me. They spoke mysteries of the precepts of God that led to His statutes and laws. They revealed another dimension to the nature of God and a new understanding of dimensional travel.

"Son, now do you see more of the 'beyond beyond' that I have been revealing to you?"

"Yes, Father, I see that reconciliation goes beyond this dimension, this time and this space continuum. Yes, I see the restoration of things beyond what I could ever imagine or think without this mantle. I see time streams and history itself having no limits and being no limitation on Your desire for restoration."

I saw that the scope of reconciliation and restoration was 'beyond beyond', but this mantle envisioned and empowered me to see and feel the cries of creation dimensionally and from my generational timelines. I also felt and sensed that the Ambassadors of the races that I had previously encountered were but the beginning of dimensional restoration.

"Yes, son, there is always more! So prepare your heart for change: engage the eternal flame once again."

The flame is to be found 'beyond': it is a representation of the process of the dark cloud experience but it is also a dimensional place.

So once again I walked beyond the throne of grace, to the doorways to 'beyond'. There at the matrix of dimensional space, at the event horizon, I was drawn to a portal with a tiny slit revolving at a very high speed. I hesitated again. How could I ever get through? I realised that what I was seeing was no physical barrier or entrance but represented my conscious mind's unwillingness to go beyond and that I had created the impenetrable appearance of this access point out of my own understanding. The way in was by desire and willingness which began to increase so that my confusion could decrease.

"Son, now that you have this realisation, there is no barrier that can resist your entering other than what your mind creates through fear. Son, you decide, you choose, now that you are free."

The revolving slit slowly transformed into a transparent but slightly diffracted energy field similar to all the other doorways I have seen. I have become aware of many more doors in this place that I could not previously see; not set out in a linear fashion but like a spirally curved maze.

Suddenly the possibilities are endless and I wait, weighing up the cost and pondering the potential adventures ahead...

Are you willing to journey to your beyond beyond?

Notes

References

1. Joff Day: *Forgive, Release and be Free*
2. C.S. Lewis: *Letters to Malcolm: Chiefly on Prayer.*
3. C.S. Lewis: *The Great Divorce.*
4. James B. Torrance, *Worship, Community and the Triune God of Grace* (Downer's Grove: IVP Academic, 1996), p34.
5. Andre Rabe, *Icons of Beauty.*
6. John Crowder, *The Great Iconoclast*, article published on www.thenewmystics.com
7. University of Southampton school of Mathematical Sciences study, published January 2017.
8. David van Koevering, *Keys to Taking Your Quantum Leap*, article published on www.elijahlist.com

Bible quotations:

Unless otherwise noted, Bible quotations are taken from the New American Standard Bible® (**NASB**): Copyright © 1960, 1962, 1963, 1968, 1971, 1972, 1973, 1975, 1977, 1995 by The Lockman Foundation. Used by permission (www.Lockman.org).

Other versions used:

AMP: Scripture taken from the Amplified Bible, Copyright © 1954, 1958, 1962, 1964, 1965, 1987 by The Lockman Foundation. Used by permission.

MEV: Scripture taken from the Modern English Version. Copyright © 2014 by Military Bible Association. Used by permission. All rights reserved.

MIR: The Mirror Bible: The Bible translated from the original text and paraphrased in contemporary speech with commentary. Copyright © 2017 by Francois du Toit. Used by kind permission of the author. All rights reserved.

NIV: Scriptures taken from the Holy Bible, New International Version®, NIV®. Copyright © 1973, 1978, 1984, 2011 by Biblica, Inc.™ Used by permission of Zondervan. All rights reserved worldwide. www.zondervan.com. The "NIV" and "New International Version" are trademarks registered in the United States Patent and Trademark Office by Biblica, Inc.™

NKJV: Scripture taken from the New King James Version®. Copyright © 1982 by Thomas Nelson. Used by permission. All rights reserved.

NLT: Scripture quotations are taken from the Holy Bible, New Living Translation, copyright ©1996, 2004, 2007, 2013 by Tyndale House Foundation. Used by permission of Tyndale House Publishers, Inc., Carol Stream, Illinois 60188. All rights reserved.

Appendix

Applying the Body and Blood of Jesus to the renewal of the mind:

I eat Your flesh and drink Your blood so that I will have the Mind of Christ.

I engage in the body and blood of Jesus and I embrace the transforming power of the Mind of Christ contained within it.

I engage the record containing the light, sound and frequency of God's consciousness for the renewal of my mind back to its eternal condition.

I embrace the record of the dimensions of the kingdom released in my mind by the thoughts of God to renew, rewire and restore my brain and thinking.

I speak to my marrow and command it to be a new source of blood that will renew and rewire the cells of my brain so that I can have the mind of Christ.

I apply the frequency of God's thoughts resonating with truth to transform my mind into the Mind of Christ by removing all lies and breaking all strongholds.

I command every neural pathway attached to negative memories and ungodly behaviours to be broken and new neural pathways aligned to truth to be formed.

I apply the blood of Jesus to all negative and impure memories and break all connections to sin and trauma – Mind and thinking, be renewed!

I apply the blood of Jesus to all negative images within my imagination and all negative belief systems within my reason centre – Mind, be cleansed!

I call my mind to resonate with the thoughts of God contained within the Mind of Christ and to come into alignment and agreement with an eternal perspective.

I trigger the ability for telepathic communication, telekinetic power and transmutation abilities.

I trigger the ability of creative thought, translation, bilocation, pre- and post-cognition, and time travel.

The Law of Deconstruction

Context:

The context is the renewal of the mind.

And do not be conformed to this world, but be transformed by the renewing of your mind... (Romans 12:2).

...and that you be renewed in the spirit of your mind (Ephesians 4:23).

The deconstruction of the mind's pillars by challenging and shaking old mind-sets with love bombs of truth.

Authority, Rights and Powers:

You are authorised to accelerate the process of cognitive dissonance.

You are authorised to release traumatic encounters that will fracture the illusions.

You are authorised to expose the old to new levels of revelation.

You are authorised to release the messenger angels to effect mind-quakes.

You are authorised to increase the intensity and pressure for transformation through facilitating deeper dimensional encounters.

Jurisdiction:

You are authorised to call for the radicalisation of the Joshua Generation by deconstruction.

Consequences:

You can expect greater opposition and a falling away of those who are not bold and courageous.

You can expect an accelerated transition for those who embrace deconstruction.

You will need trauma centres, places of rehabilitation for the deconstructed and deprogrammed.

Law of Fatherhood and Sonship

I decree in the court of Kings the law of fatherhood and sonship.

I call forth the spirit that turns the hearts of the children back to their Father.

I call forth a new dimension in intimacy and relationship in sonship.

I call forth the alignment in the spirit with the 4 faces of God.

I call forth a new dimension in the revelation of ministry in that alignment: King – Prophet – Apostle – Priest.

I decree a new foundational government be established by resonating with the sound frequency of heaven that is calling for restoration.

I decree a new kingdom government and a new season where lords rise up, take their heavenly positions and responsibilities, and establish the new.

Legislation for the Depth of the Father's Heart

You are authorised to release a new wave of intimacy.

You are authorised to call for deep to call for deep.

You are authorised to rip open the hearts of men with the power of love.

You are authorised to call to orphans to come home into the adoption of sonship.

You are authorised to call for the removal of masks that hide the orphan spirit.

You are authorised to call for open heart surgery to remove the hardness of damaged hearts.

You are authorised to undo the yokes and remove the heavy burdens of the slavery mentality.

You are authorised to release the love of the Father to broken hearts.

You are authorised to pour out the balm of the Father's heart to heal brokenness.

You are authorised to administrate the eternal love of God to call My people back to their eternal identity as sons of light.

The Law of New Beginnings

Son, you are hereby authorised to release the law of new beginnings. You are authorised to legislate for and on behalf of the Joshua Generation to release sonship to answer creation's groan.

I establish the law of new beginnings.

This law can only be legislated by sons of the order of Melchizedek in the Joshua Generation.

Sons, you are authorised to answer creation's groan.

Sons, you are authorised to create new blueprints for restoration of the created order.

Sons, you are authorised to create the fabric of the third age creation.

Sons, you are to go beyond creation and recreation to bring the order of the new third day.

Sons, you are authorised to subdue and rule to establish synchronicity with creation.

Sons, you are authorised to open the house of discoveries and release the organics needed for the dawn of the third day.

Sons, you are authorised to administrate the rising of the mountain of the house of the Lord.

Sons, you are authorised to complete the circle where precepts meet precepts and the Treasury House is fully open and operational.

Sons, you are authorised to align the beginning and end of the third day with the ages to come.

Sons of maturity will be mandate-completers and will be entrusted to access the pillars of wisdom to release the creative blueprints that align the third day of the old age with the first day of the new age to come.

Sons, time and space of the old age must be brought back under the rule of sonship so that a new convergence of the spheres can usher in a new space-time continuum.

Sons, you have been called to take your places in the councils and assemblies of creative authority; now mature and grow up.

Sons, the restoration of all things has been placed in your hands, the restoration of what was intended to be in the convergence of time and eternity. You must expand your conscious reality to extend beyond creation and recreation to the new creation reality of the sons of God.

Legislation for the Removal of Restrictions

I call for the removal of the limits to unveil the beyond, the limitless potential possibilities of eternal reality.

I call for freedom from the religious restrictions that are creating limitations.

I call for justice against all the fear-based entanglements that are hindering the exchange.

I call the heavenly hosts to witness for justice that all mind-sets of limitation will be exposed and removed from the councils of 3, 7, 12, and all mountain benches.

I call for the courage and boldness to possess the unknown to be instilled into hearts and minds.

I call for all selfishness to be exposed and surrendered.

I call for hearts, minds and wills to be filled with compassion, zeal and passion.

I call for all confusion to be removed from hearts and minds.

I call for all obstacles to be removed from those who will be drawn to the light.

I call for the mountains to be made low and the valleys to be lifted up, the rough places to be made smooth and the crooked paths to be made straight.

I call for the opening of the everlasting doors and for the atmosphere to be cleansed.

I call for the angelic armies to be released with fire into the atmosphere over our footprint.

Keep up to date with
Mike's personal journey
'beyond beyond'.

Subscribe to his
YouTube channel at
freedomarc.org/youtube

Follow Freedom ARC
on social media:

freedomarc.org/facebook

freedomarc.org/twitter

freedomarc.org/instagram

freedomarc.org/pinterest

and on our *Sons of Issachar* blog:

www.freedomarc.blog

You'll find links to these and
much more on our website:

www.freedomarc.org

CPSIA information can be obtained
at www.ICGtesting.com
Printed in the USA
BVHW07s0925280918
528763BV00001B/1/P